PRAISE FOR *MANAGING THE MILLENNIALS*

"If you're going to run a successful organization in the future, you'll have to learn how to manage the Millennial generation—that thundering herd of young people whose numbers exceed the Baby Boomers. They will push you and frustrate you, but they will help you win going forward. Managing the Millennials *is a must-read for every leader who wants his or her organization to have a great future."*
—Ken Blanchard, coauthor of *The One Minute Manager*®
  and *Leading at a Higher Level*

"Our company has had the good fortune of becoming a trusted brand with the new generation. Without them, we would not exist. It would be easy for us to think that we "know enough" because of our business. The truth is that we cannot afford to not build the same trust within our organization between the generations that make up the Quiksilver family. Managing the Millennials *is a practical hands-on approach to understanding how generational tension gets created and what to do about it. I was fascinated by what I learned and excited about sharing it within our company."*
—Robert McKnight, Founder and CEO, Quiksilver, Inc.

*"*Managing the Millennials *has taught us how to harvest the creativity and energy of a new generation and inspire those of us who lead them."*
—Bruce Ratner, CEO, Forest City Ratner Companies,
  and Principal Owner, NBA New Jersey Nets

"With more than 32 million twenty-somethings in today's workforce, managers more than ever before need a clear road map for building bridges of communication and engagement between generations. Based on years of research and real-world business experience, Managing the Millennials *is the first book to fuse the authors' cutting-edge concepts with a powerful and easy-to-use framework for putting their ideas into action. This is one book that I will wholeheartedly recommend to every business leader whose job includes managing people."*
—Peter Economy, best-selling author of *Managing For Dummies*,
  and Associate Editor, *Leader to Leader* magazine

"This book is timely and practical for those facing the challenge of managing across generations. It takes a certain degree of maturity and perspective to be able to suspend one's own bias and engage others. Managers who practice the core competencies in this book will be better equipped to develop the people they lead."
—Laura Curnutt Santana, PhD, Senior Enterprise Associate,
  Center for Creative Leadership

"For any leader who is interested in passing along a legacy to future generations, Managing the Millennials *is a must-read. This book provides practical instruction on how to relationally connect with the growing and influential workforce that will one day run the world, emphasizing a mature approach to coaching and relating—while realizing the potential for change in yourself in the process. I'm confident you will enjoy reading it, just as I did."*
—Patrick McClenahan, President/General Manager, CBS2/KCAL9, Los Angeles, CA

"As a legacy organization, we are concerned about who will carry the torch of Special Olympics forward. Our mission is relevant as ever but we really believe our future is dependent upon a new generation of athletes, coaches, volunteers, and staff grasping the vision. Managing the Millennials *has helped our leadership team understand how to engage Millennials in the present so that we can count on them in the future."*
—Bill Shumard, President, Special Olympics Southern California

Managing the
Millennials

Managing the Millennials

Discover the
Core Competencies for
Managing Today's Workforce

CHIP ESPINOZA

MICK UKLEJA

CRAIG RUSCH

WILEY

John Wiley & Sons, Inc.

Published by John Wiley & Sons, Inc., Hoboken, New Jersey.

Published simultaneously in Canada.

For general information on our other products and services or for technical support, please contact our Customer Care Department within the United States at (800) 762-2974, outside the United States at (317) 572-3993 or fax (317) 572-4002.

Wiley also publishes its books in a variety of electronic formats. Some content that appears in print may not be available in electronic books. For more information about Wiley products, visit our web site at www.wiley.com.

Library of Congress Cataloging-in-Publication Data:
Espinoza, Chip, 1962-
   Managing the millennials : discover the core competencies for managing today's workforce / Chip Espinoza, Mick Ukleja, Craig Rusch.
   p. cm.
   Includes bibliographical references and index.
   ISBN 978-0-470-56393-9 (cloth)
   1. Personnel management. 2. Management. 3. Intergenerational communication. 4. Intergenerational relations. 5. Young adults—Employment. 6. Generation X—Employment. 7. Generation Y—Employment.
   I. Ukleja, Mick. II. Rusch, Craig, 1964- III. Title.
   HF5549.E796 2010
   658.30084'2—dc22

                                                                   2009041469

Printed in the United States of America

15 14 13 12 11 10

CONTENTS

CONTENTS

FOREWORD

CAMERON JOHNSON, TELEVISION PERSONALITY AND AUTHOR OF YOU CALL THE SHOTS

Growing up as a young entrepreneur, I've seen the generational differences in the business world first-hand. I started my first business when I was nine years old and before my 21st birthday, I had started more than a dozen profitable businesses. I was able to do this, two ways: by leveraging technology and by also quickly learning the generational differences.

I was able to find customers from more than sixty countries, manage employees who were sometimes more than triple my age, and to do so efficiently —as I was, of course, still in school. I'm now 25, and I'm seeing my peers enter a workforce that is very different, very different from what they expected that is.

I've heard my generation referred to as "The Entitlement Generation", "Generation Me", "Generation Debt"—and quite frankly, I don't disagree with any of them. My generation grew up with the latest and greatest technological advancements of the past century. We've grown up with iPods, cell phones, computers, and don't let me forget, the Internet. We're a generation in which

"I don't know" isn't in our vocabulary, as the answer is always just a search away.

More kids are graduating college than ever before, which means more competition for the graduate, but also an even better pool of applicants for your company. Technology has enabled companies to become even more efficient as the access to information has become easier, cheaper, and faster. Efficiency is the key to success within any company, and I also believe it's the key to unlocking the power of my generation.

There are already more than 32 million Millennials in the workforce and most likely some in your company today. This means opportunity for you. Opportunity to leverage us to maximize our potential and most importantly, to maximize what we can do for you and in your company.

Chip, Mick, and Craig have done just that in this fantastic book. *Managing the Millennials* answers your questions and provides solutions for integrating this new generation into your business. I found the research and insight in the pages ahead to be invaluable and I think you'll agree.

—Cameron Johnson
  Television Personality and Author, *You Call the Shots*
  www.cameronjohnson.com
  December 2009

ACKNOWLEDGMENTS

The three of us would like to thank Dr. Joel Schwarzbart for his enormous support. His influence, insight, and intellect can be found throughout this book. Thank you to Mark Stump for helping to coordinate our effort. We would also like to thank the Margret McBride Literary Agency team for its belief in our work and the impact it will make in organizations.

Thank you to my wife Lisa and our four children (Chase, Chance, Chandler, and Charlize). They are my inspiration. Thank you to Cholene Espinoza and Ellen Ratner for their encouragement, confidence, and ideas.

Thank you to Dr. Norman Shawchuck and Dr. Roger Heuser for teaching me to ask why before how. Thank you to Dr. Al Guskin, faculty, and fellow students of Antioch University's PhD. in Leadership and Change Program for guiding my thinking through this project.

Thank you to the students in my Management 470 class for challenging me as much as I challenged them.

—*Chip Espinoza*

Thank you to my wife Louise for her unwavering support over the years. I appreciate the insights she brings to each project. Thank you to my son Mark who is a young GenX(er), his wife Amy, and my daughter Michelle who is a Millennial for showing me the bias of my own experience. They have given me a new lens through which to understand generational differences and the values that drive them.

Thank you to David and Brian Lucas and the Bonita Bay Group for their support and participation in the development stages of our ideas.

Thank you to Dr. Ken Blanchard for his support and critique of the development of this book. Thank you to my former co-author and good friend Dr. Robert Lorber who allowed us access to his clients for our research.

—*Mick Ukleja*

Thank you to Eric and Candice, my Millennial children for your love and support. Thank you to Dr. Ed Clarke, chair of the department of anthropology and sociology, Dr. Daniel de Roulet, and Dr. James Huff for supporting this project and sharing early drafts in a Vanguard University faculty reading group. Thank you to Dr. Julie Howard, Dr. John Wilson, Claudia Degelman, Cheryl Jensen, and Jed McClure for offering in-depth feedback.

Thank you to Dean Mayeda, Tom Slowey, Scott Ruther, Joe Stoudt, Ginger and David Kricorian, Dr. Gerard Beenen, and Dr. Tim Moyers for your encouragement through the research and development process. Finally, thank you to all of my students.

—*Craig Rusch*

INTRODUCTION

CLOSE ENCOUNTERS WITH A DIFFERENT KIND

Raise your hand if you have ever had an encounter at work with a younger employee that left you completely puzzled. Relax, you are not alone!

There are currently four generations at work (Builders, Baby Boomers, GenX, and Millennials), and three of the generations have been playing nice together for well over a decade. Therefore, our attention will focus on where most of the angst lies—between the new kids on the block (Millennials) and the other age cohorts.

We are constantly amazed at how the topic of "Managing the Millennials" resonates with people. Standing in line for a latte, on a plane, or at a cocktail party, when we talk about our research, it creates a buzz. Although interested in hearing about our findings, people are even more eager to tell their own story. Odds are that if you bought this book, you have your own story. You have lived it, and you have experienced the tension.

A few years ago, we began to notice a growing frustration among managers and business leaders with integrating younger workers into their organizations. Activities that in the past had been relatively straightforward—like recruiting, retaining, and rewarding—now seemed more challenging than ever; and we were not the only ones who noticed. Newspapers, journals, magazines, niche publications, *60 Minutes*, and even movies have captured the phenomena of the Millennial in the workplace. The stories portrayed reactions that ranged from amazement to incredulity to outrage. These reactions are the result of values and behaviors exhibited by Millennial employees, which cause them to appear distinctly different from their vocational forerunners and which are undermining norms that have supported the workplace for decades.

This book is the result of a two-year study to find out how managers can be successful with their Millennial employees in the face of these challenges. We wanted to "get inside" the relational dynamics. Our objective was to identify behaviors and traits exhibited by Millennials that managers deemed problematic. We interviewed hundreds of managers and employees in a variety of work environments. Data from the interviews were used to build a model, which we explain in the following chapters. The model illustrates the different values held by each generation. It also shows how behaviors exhibited by the holders of those values are often misperceived, and how those misperceptions in turn lead to inter-generational tension. We explain why generations have differing values and how such values manifest through behaviors and interactions that create tension in the workplace.

Specifically, we identify nine points of tension that result from clashing value systems in a cross-generational management context, and nine competencies required to mitigate each counterproductive disconnect. We have committed a chapter to each of the competencies. Each chapter describes the tension, potential disconnect, and the competency that leads to generational rapport. Our mission is not just to describe the conflict. We go beyond that to provide tools for resolving the tension that inhibits the success of both managers and Millennials.

If you are a reader of management literature then you are familiar with many of the managerial leader practices in the following pages. Some practices are familiar while others are novel, but all have received respect in academic and practitioner literatures. However, concepts and models are only helpful if you know where and how to apply them. The value of our work is to help you identify the areas that can undermine your success as a manager and what to do about these areas. Most of the managers who have attended our workshops have commented that *Managing the Millennials* is useful for managing all ages. We agree. As it happens, the solutions that we share include best practices that can be applied in many relational settings. However, there is special urgency in the multigenerational context, and especially so with Millennial employees.

Demographers William Strauss and Neil Howe reference the *Harry Potter* series as an excellent illustration for the differences between Millennials and their predecessors (Builders, Baby Boomers, and GenX). Harry Potter and his friends are smart, over achieving, innovative, and self-possessed, doing their best to operate within the rules set forth for them, while practicing their calling of saving the world as need arises—they represent Millennials. The individualistic, judgmental, egotistical teachers at Hogwarts responsible for shaping the young wizards characterize the Baby Boomer generation. Characters like Hagrid, though not in power but always around to help, epitomize Generation X—a group sandwiched between two powerful and dominant generations.

Unlike any other generation before them, Millennials are the first generation that can access information without an authority figure. They are wizards with technology, visionaries with high expectations; armed with knowledge or the know-how to access it, they proclaim themselves as ready. Ready for any challenge, ready for more responsibility, and, as John Mayer sings, "Waiting on the world to change." They perceive themselves to be "in waiting," held back by well-meaning elders whose best years have come and gone. Millennials respect their elders for what they have done but relegate their future utility to the role of mentor, career counselor, and cheerleader.

At the core of the Millennial phenomenon is that they do not have the same need or know-how to build relationships with their managers or authority figures. Previous generations had to take initiative to relationally connect in order to gain information and access. It is a natural arrangement that has played itself out for generations. Things are different now. The rules have changed. A Millennial with a wireless laptop can usurp the authority of a decorated professor in her own classroom. Builders, Baby Boomers, and GenX cannot help but sense the shift, "Why don't they ever come and ask me questions?" We suggest that either they do not think they need to or they do not know how. The dichotomy is that they desperately want mentors or career advocates. That leads us to believe that most Millennials just do not know how to relate to someone who is in authority that is not already perceived to be "for" them.

The other side of the coin is that managers do not recall the experience of their superiors reaching out to them. It is a behavior they do not remember being modeled to them. They know why and how to reach upward but do not feel the need to reach downward or they just do not know how. And for good reason, traditional managerial leader training programs focus on how managers can get subordinates to do what she or he wants them to do. One of the first questions that surfaces from an audience is, "How can you help me change them [the Millennials]."

Although we devote a great deal of attention to the values, attitudes, and behaviors of Millennial employees, our story is not about them. The lead character in our story is the manager—the person responsible for the productivity of, development of, and knowledge transfer to the emerging workforce. In the chapters that follow, we characterize how the managers in our study experience Millennials on the job. The managers and leaders we worked with expressed both admiration and frustration. We preserved their expressions unedited in order to illustrate both the barriers to and opportunities for adaptation, engagement, and communication. Because the manager's expressions are unedited, we have chosen to omit their names in an effort to provide anonymity. You notice that we do not use company names. Companies are often used to promote and legitimize managerial concepts. Our work is legitimized by the everyday experiences of managers. This book challenges both how you think about management and how you manage. Those who are willing to adapt will reap great benefits both personally and professionally.

Understandably, many managers are reluctant to take on the added burden of learning and practicing a new set of skills required to be adaptive to the challenges presented by Millennial employees. One of the more frequent refrains we heard from managers who were reluctant to accept this burden was, "They [Millennials] just need to grow up—just like any other generation."

The most important question in this book can only be answered by you—are you willing to adapt? When it comes to managing Millennials, it is our belief that the people with the most maturity will have to adapt first. We are saying that you are the key to your own success, your organization's success, and ultimately the success of the Millennials.

As a point of clarification, we acknowledge that managing and leading are two different functions, but because they often are performed by the same person, we use the terms interchangeably.

PART

I

THE MILLENNIALS HAVE ARRIVED!

CHAPTER

1

THE MILLENNIALS AND YOU

If we don't like a job, we quit, because the worst thing that can happen is that we move back home. There's no stigma, and many of us grew up with both parents working, so our moms would love nothing more than to cook our favorite meatloaf.

—Jason Ryan Dorsey (28 years old)[1]

Have you noticed a recent change in your workplace? Young people—particularly members of a new generation of workers that we refer to as Millennials—are joining our workforce. Are you ready for them? And have you noticed that they are a little different than you? You might even think they are strange or that they do not quite have "it" together. Maybe they sometimes show up to work wearing flip-flops, or they have iPod headphones hanging from their ears. And perhaps they just sit at their desks waiting for someone to give them something to do. Let us be the first to tell you that the invasion of Millennials will soon become a flood. In 2006, Millennials comprised 21 percent of the workforce—nearly 32 million workers.[2] Over the next decade they will be *all in*! Successful managers will be the ones who understand, appreciate, and learn to work with the differences in values, work-life priorities, and expectations they bring.

The Millennial flood has become front-page news—virtually every form of media is talking about it, from mainline television news channels to newspapers to niche magazines and journals. *USA Today* had this to say on the topic: "Businesses are struggling to keep pace with a new generation of young people entering the workforce who have starkly different attitudes and desires than employees over the past few decades." *Human Resource Executive* says, "Millennials, people in their twenties, are just now entering the workforce bringing with them new promises and challenges for HR, not to mention a whole new way of working." Clearly, something has changed from previous generations to this newest generation of *twentysomethings*, and management is worried that the change is not all good.

Let us say that you run a corporation—who is going to take over for you when you're gone? Do you think the next generation is ready to take over? Or perhaps you run a family business—do you think your kids are ready to step into that role? Guess what—*today is the tomorrow you worried about yesterday*. It is here. Now. The aliens have landed. Remember those old science fiction movies from the 1950s? These beings would climb out of their spaceships that flew halfway across the galaxy to pay us a visit. They looked just like humans, but there was something different, something not quite right. Some people thought these aliens were hostile when in actuality they came in peace.

The new generation of twentysomethings has seen the help-wanted signs in our windows. They know we really need them—and guess what? They need us just as much as we need them. So the thing to do is to reach out and get to know them. What motivates them? What do they think? How do they learn? What do they expect? Why reach out? Because we each have what the other really wants and needs, and because our success—and the success of our organizations—depends upon it.

THE GENERATIONS AT WORK

But aren't all youth the same? The answer to that is yes and no. There are some common characteristics of all youth, whether they were born a hundred years ago or just a decade ago. Before we address whether all youth are the same, let's briefly outline the four generations currently in the workplace.

In our training sessions, we do an exercise where we break into groups and have the participants talk about the clothing they wore, the music they listened to, the sociopolitical events they remember, and the technology they used in their adolescence and young adulthood. You can imagine how quickly people start to compare their experiences. In one of our sessions, a Builder, a person born from 1925 through the end of World War II to 1945, told of how her family shared a telephone with other families in the area. Few people today remember that they were referred to as "party lines." A Millennial pulled a smart phone out of his pocket and said, "This is my party line. I can connect to five people at once."

The Builders

There were 56 million Builders. The Great Depression, Roosevelt's New Deal, the Korean War, World War II, the GI Bill—all left an indelible stamp on the members of this generation. As a result of the GI Bill, 49 percent of those admitted into college in 1947 were veterans. By 1956, nearly eight million World War II veterans had taken advantage of the opportunity to further their education.[3] Authority was important as was hard work, honor, and delayed gratification. People were willing to work 30 years or more before they got their gold watch and could retire. It was not uncommon to spend one's entire career at one company.

The Baby Boomers

Then along came the next generation—the Baby Boomers—born from 1946 to 1964, numbering 80 million or so men and women. Vietnam, the Cold War, the Civil Rights Movement, the Women's

Liberation Movement, television, and rock and roll all made an indelible impression on this generation. The Baby Boomers protested in favor of equality for everybody, and they discovered the charms of credit cards (which drove their Builder parents crazy—they remembered the Depression and learned the lesson not to buy on credit). The Kennedy and King assassinations robbed them of their innocence, while the moon landing showed the world they could do anything they set their minds to. For the Baby Boomers, values such as professional identity, health and wellness, and material wealth are all very important. Boomers are forever young—run fast, jump long, and throw hard. They wanted free drugs in the 1960s and now they want free drugs again, this time from Medicare. Because they find much of their identity in their work, it is no surprise that Baby Boomers have added one month per year to the workweek. When it comes to technology, they use it to do *more* work—not less.

Generation X

Then along came another group—Generation X—born from 1965 to 1977, which numbers 38 million. GenX(ers) were influenced by more recent events such as the Persian Gulf War, the Challenger explosion, AIDS, corporate downsizing, a tripling of the divorce rate, both parents working (latchkey kids), video games, MTV, computers—all made their mark on this generation. They were suspicious of their parents. They say, "Wait a minute. You mean you can land a man on the moon, and yet you can't even get a rocket off the launch pad?" Some of the values that emerged from their experience include mobility and autonomy. They need to be able to move around and want to be their own person. Their greatest value is to have balance in their lives. Technology came of age, and the members of this generation use it for work-life balance. They don't perceive a need to be in the office—they could sit on the beach and do their work.

The Millennials

Today there's a new generation known as Generation Y or the Millennials. Demographers place their birth years between 1978 and 1996. There are 78 million *twentysomethings* and they make up more than 25 percent of this country's population. They have been shaped by 9/11 and terrorism, Columbine (which took the King and Kennedy assassinations to a new and more personal level), the girl's movement—Spice Girls, Dixie Chicks, cell phones, text messaging, technology-based social networking, and a strong emphasis on social responsibility.

Technology isn't a tool to just do more work or to achieve work-life balance—it is an integral part of the members of this group, and working with it has become second nature. The members of this new generation want and need constant feedback. Why? Because they were raised in democratic and praise-based families that proudly displayed "My kid made the honor roll" bumper stickers. They grew up in an era where the focus of parenting was nurturing. They have grown up working on teams in school and on academic projects. When they get into the workforce, they expect to work in teams. Diversity is important to them. If they walk into the workplace and don't see diversity, they think something is wrong. What about morality? Abstinence is up. Substance abuse is down. Youth today, more than ever, are interested in developing their spirituality.

The O Generation

The O Generation clock started in 1997 and will continue into the second decade of the twenty-first century. The forerunners in the group are turning 12 years old. They will be coming of age during the Obama presidency. Their cohort will be smaller than that of the Millennials. Here are some of the things that may impact their values and attitudes; Mortgage Crisis, Corporate Bailouts, Hannah Montana, "Sully" and US Airways Flight 1549, "Captain Phillips" thwarts Somalian Pirates, and the Obama Election and Presidency.

THE COMING JOB GAP

There is a global phenomenon taking place. It is called global aging, and its impact will be evident over the next few years.

Domestic supplies of labor will decline in many developed countries or will grow at a markedly reduced rate compared with previous generations. Large numbers of the most experienced workers will exit the labor force due to retirement and mortality. The battle for talent will intensify within regions. Countries will battle for dwindling supplies of indigenous, high-skilled labor. The European Union alone is currently experiencing a 25 percent decline in population.[4] The Great Recession of 2008 to 2009 has temporarily slowed the exit of Baby Boomers from the workforce, but the exodus will resume once the economy—and retirement savings—recover.

At least 50 percent of executives in the United States will be eligible to retire in the next five years.[5] You might think, "Well, that's okay. We'll just let the people in the next positions take their place." The problem is that the people in the second, third, and fourth positions are also Baby Boomers, and they're going to be retiring, too. Long story short, an organization's future vitality is dependent on its ability to attract, retain, motivate, and develop Millennials.

Millennials are the most socially and diversely tolerant generation ever, the most educated and technologically savvy generation ever, and also the most sheltered and structured generation in our country's history. One in three is not Caucasian. One in four comes from a single-parent home. Three in four have working mothers; and in two-parent homes, children get more time with parents than they did 25 years ago.[6] Naturally, they comprise the fastest-growing segment of the workforce. There are currently more than 32 million twentysomething workers in the United States and that number will continue to grow through the year 2015.

YOU'RE SO SPECIAL

There are six major value-shaping influences that impact every generation as its members move through their formative years:

family, education, morality, peers, spirituality, and culture. Let us examine how a few of these influences have shaped Millennials—in forming their value system, their worldview, and their aspirations in life.

While Baby Boomers live to work, Millennials work to live. For Baby Boomers, authority and hierarchy are important. For Millennials, not so much. They don't care what your title is—they want to know if you have the goods. When it comes to salary and wealth, Baby Boomers are convinced they need to work hard to earn it. Millennials simply expect it. Baby Boomers believe in position, performance, and individual reward. Millennials? Again, not so much.

From an early age, Millennials were taught that they were special. The self-esteem movement caught hold in the 1980s. Its aim was to build self-confidence in children by taking a more nurturing approach to early education. Researchers who study the rise of narcissism in the United States, like Jean Twenge of San Diego State University, believe the self-esteem movement may have gone too far.[7] One of the examples Twenge cites is a song commonly sung in preschools. The words "I am special, I am special. Look at me" are sung to the tune of "Frere Jacques." Catalogs of books and other media for teachers are filled with titles that include the phrases "I am special," "all about me," "celebrate me," "the poem of me," and so on.

But just how special are these young men and women? Consider these direct, unedited quotes from people who manage Millennials.

- "They do not care about customers."

- "If you correct them, they quit."

- "They think there is always an excuse that can make being late okay."

- "They want a trophy for just showing up."

- "Yelling and screaming is the only thing they understand."

- "They pick up computer and cash register skills quickly, but if it breaks they cannot count back change from a $10 bill."

- "She asked for an extended lunch hour to go shopping with friends after her third day on the job."

- "They assume it is okay to call me by my first name like we are buddies. I am their boss."

- "Anything extra nice I do, they act as if I owed it to them."

But what about Millennials' perceptions of themselves? As you see in the following direct quotes, their perceptions of themselves are not inconsistent with the perceptions of others.

- "We are not defined by our job."

- "We want to have a say about when we work."

- "We want to have a say about how we do our work."

- "We do not expect you to be our best friend, but when you evaluate or critique us, we want you to do it in a friendly way (just like their parents did)."

- "We want you to give us direction and then get out of our way."

Millennials have high perceptions of themselves. They think that they work better and faster than other workers. They have high expectations of their employers, and they want direct and fair input from managers. They want managers to be involved in their professional development, because it is all about them in many ways—it is not just about the company. They seek out creative challenges and view peers as vast resources from whom to gain knowledge. They want to be recognized and valued the first day on the job. They want small goals with tight deadlines so they can see their own development as they slowly take ownership of a new role. In summary, Millennials are high performance (with a lot of potential) and high maintenance. For many managers, the maintenance clouds the potential. Instead of opportunity and promise, they see a headache.

BRIDGING THE GAP

Here's the rub. More than 60 percent of employers say that they are experiencing tension between employees from different generations—more than 70 percent of older employees are dismissive of younger workers' abilities. If this were not bad enough, 50 percent of younger employees are dismissive of the abilities of their older coworkers.[8] The tension is so thick in some organizations that it has become debilitating.

An organization's future vitality is dependent on its ability to work with Millennials. Many managerial leaders are beginning to recognize this fact, and they are taking action now to bridge the gap between the generations. The emphasis on recruiting, employee engagement, and talent pipeline is resounding throughout conference rooms across the country. According to Scott Pollack at PricewaterhouseCoopers, the story does not end with recruiting. Says Pollack, "The war for talent has shifted. You still want to recruit, but the new challenge is, how do you keep the best people?"

Today, retaining the best people is key to competitive advantage. Do not let the current down cycle in employment fool you. Millennial employees are going to have almost unlimited opportunities for work—from sea to shining sea. What are you going to do to attract them, keep them, and unleash their creativity and energy? Okay, Millennials have a different set of attitudes, values, and beliefs than do the men and women who preceded them into the workplace. You have a choice: You can *villainize* them and say, "They just aren't the way we used to be." Or you can *tolerate* them and say, "We have no choice. We have to let them work here." Or you can *engage* them, and benefit from the contribution they will make.

So the ultimate question is this: How are we going to manage differently? In the chapters that follow, we explore this question—and the answers to it—in great detail.

CHAPTER

2

AREN'T WE ALL JUST THE SAME?

Society persists despite the mortality of its individual members, through process of demographic metabolism and particularly the annual infusion of birth cohorts. These may pose a threat to stability, but they also provide the opportunity for societal transformation.

—Norman Ryder

SO WHAT? ISN'T EVERY GENERATION THE SAME?

When speaking about our research, we often face skeptics who ask, "Aren't Millennials the same as every other generation? Don't they challenge the status quo, push boundaries, and engage in an experimental lifestyle just as every generation did in its youth?"[1] The answer to the second question is obviously "yes," but that does not mean the answer to the first is too. Separating these two questions allows us to provide a useful response.

Sometimes the best answer to a question is another question. Think about this: Due to technology, Millennials are the first generation that does not need an authority figure to access information. Do you think that may shape how they relate to authority figures or how tacit knowledge gets transferred?

Maturational Theory

An obvious starting point for giving a meaningful answer to our skeptics is with *maturational theory*, the traditional belief that people change, mature, and develop their values, attitudes, and preferences as a function of age. As visual acuity, crawling, walking, and speaking are all the normative result of growing up or aging, so are attitudes and values. By observing the maturing process, we build expectations with respect to events like a child taking her first step, uttering his first word, or "knowing better."

Arnold Gesell established the concept of *developmental norms* in his quest to understand by what age a certain attitude or behavior should generally be observable. If a child at age four tells tall tales, the parent must recognize the nature of the child's immaturity and not be alarmed. Who hasn't been warmed by a small child's imaginative fibs? But when the child is age 16, we are no longer inclined to be entertained. Instead of characterizing the utterances as "imaginative" or calling them "fibs," concerned parents will try to determine the appropriate punishment for the lie. Gesell viewed biological development as the major determinant to behavior.[2]

Generational Theory

It is true that *all generations* exhibit characteristics of youth, but their values and attitudes about work and life depend on so much more. Take, for instance, the questions of what are the appropriate ages to move out of a parent's home, get married, and start a career. We argue that the answers to such questions lie beyond *maturational theory*.

Why is it that one generation considers a 25-year-old still living at home as unthinkable and another considers it normal? Why is one generation more comfortable than another with the concept of stay-at-home dads? Why are Builders likely to have had one career and labored for one or two companies their entire work life, while Baby Boomers are reported as having as many as three careers and more likely to change companies than their predecessors?

In 1981, Baby Boomer Howard Schultz was making more than $70,000 a year as a salesman for Hammarplast AB, a Swedish conglomerate that manufactures plastics for home and medical use. Schultz left his stable and successful position at Hammarplast to work for a two-store coffee enthusiast hangout in Seattle. Today, thanks to Schultz's vision and leadership, Starbucks has more than 20,000 outlets worldwide and is one of the most recognizable brands in the world. At the time Schultz made his transition, however, his mother thought he was crazy. Playing her part, she dutifully advised him, "Don't give it up for a small company no one has ever heard of!"[3] Stability and company loyalty are high values for Builders like those whose worldviews were shaped by experiencing the Great Depression in their formative years. But the work world has changed even more since Schultz's early career. Today college career counselors are advising tomorrow's workers that they can expect to have as many as five to seven careers and to labor for several companies during their work stint.

It is fascinating that each generation has a set of values, attitudes, and beliefs that inform their behavior. It is not merely a function of getting older. It is also a function of culture.

German sociologist Karl Mannheim is credited with establishing *generational theory,* which seeks to explain how attitudes and values are shaped in both individuals and groups. Mannheim thought that the generation a person belongs to determines, to a certain extent, his or her thoughts, feelings, and even behaviors. A generation is defined as a group that shares birth years and significant life events at critical developmental stages. Youth is the key period in which social generations are formed.[4] The major events experienced during the time of formation are what shapes the outlook on the world exhibited by that generation. Another term for Mannheim's *generation* is *age cohort*. In the sociological literature, the terms *generation* and *cohort* are often used interchangeably.

The passing of time as experienced in a sociological context facilitates a keen sense of generation. Christopher Bollas explains, "They can define it clearly, differentiate it from older and younger generations, and in some respects analyze why their generation is the way it is."[5] Consequently, Builders, Baby Boomers, and GenX(ers) can easily and readily identify what is different between their age cohort and others. It is not until one becomes conscious of generational difference that one can develop genuine relationships between generations.[6]

Life Course Theory

Life Course Theory is a multidisciplinary human development theory that is complemented by generational theory. In Life Course Theory, demographers, historians, developmental psychologists, and sociologists look for *cohort effects*. People who experience a sociological context at a similar age are likely to forge a perspective or mind-set that stays with them throughout their entire life.[7] Examples of historical events that had powerful cohort effects are: the Great Depression, WWII, the Beatles, the Kennedy and King assassinations, the Vietnam War, the Sexual Revolution, Women's Liberation, Watergate, the fall of the Berlin Wall, the explosion of the Columbia space shuttle, the Columbine massacre, and most recently, the first African-American elected to be President of the United States. All events are social markers that frame life experience and shape values, beliefs, and attitudes.

Whose death is more emotionally impacting—Elvis's or Michael Jackson's? Your answer will probably have more to do with your cohort effect than with the number of albums sold, concerts given, movies made, or net worth accumulated by either person. One cable news network juxtaposed the attention focused on Michael Jackson's passing with the media coverage of 20 American soldiers who lost their lives over the same period of time. The network anchor asserted that the soldiers' giving of their lives for our freedom deserved more attention than Jackson's death. While the point is well taken, the media attention was actually a socio-logical phenomena rather than a referendum on whose life was more significant. The preoccupation people had with Jackson's death was more about their own life, experience, and memories than about his. This is referred to as cohort effect.

Collective Memories

Though published in 1988 by *American Sociological Review,* Howard Schuman and Jacqueline Scott shed further light on the Jackson phenomena in a research article entitled *Generations and Collective Memories. Collective memories* is a term used to describe memories of a shared past that are retained by members of a group, large or small, that experienced it. The authors asked 1,410 Americans, 18 years and older, to think of "national or world events or changes" that have occurred over the past 50 years and to name one or two that seem to have been especially important to them. The survey found that memories of important political events and social changes are structured by age, and that adolescence and early adulthood is the primary period for generational imprinting in the sense of sociopolitical memories.

The authors' presupposition is that people will tend not to recall as important those events and changes that preceded their own lifetime. They take a developmental psychology lens and view youth as a kind of "critical period" for learning about the larger society. The authors also expected that most people will tend not to recall as important those events and changes that occur after their early adulthood. Therefore, the events that register most strongly during adolescence and early adulthood have the greater impact or influence in one's life.

Each age cohort tends to develop its own characteristic patterns of attitudes and expectations about what is and is not possible to achieve in life, about what is good and what is bad, and about whom to trust and what to fear. As an example, Generation X is the first generation in recent history that did not expect to be more affluent than its parents. Baby Boomers feared that their leaders would be assassinated, while Millennials fear that their friends will be assassinated. Builders trusted that their companies would take care of them if they were loyal.

"A cohort's size relative to the sizes of its neighbors is a persistent and compelling feature of its lifetime environment. As the new cohort reaches each major juncture in the life cycle, society has the problem of assimilating it."[8] Social change is partly the result of successive generations making their way and ultimately adapting formal and informal institutions to their way of seeing and working with the world. Sonia Austrian suggests, "People in successive cohorts or generations grow up and grow old in different ways because the surrounding sociological structures are changing. That is, the process of aging from birth to death is not entirely fixed by biology, but is influenced by changing structures and roles in which people lead their lives. The interplay between individual age and social change is *cohort flow*."[9] Members of successive cohorts age in new ways and therefore contribute to changes in the social structure.

Group and Age Norm Theory

The book's opening sentence asked if you had ever been puzzled by an encounter you had with someone from a different generation. Perhaps your experience was someone telling you rather than asking you when he or she was going to be taking time off. Maybe he or she spent an hour surfing the Web for a minor detail when the person could have solved the problem in a minute by simply picking up the telephone. Better yet, the person did not understand why you made him or her stay the whole day in the office even though he or she had completed the work.

The puzzlement is a result of not having a frame of reference for interpreting Millennial behavior. You *know* "what is acceptable" or "not acceptable" when you have been a part of establishing expectations. For the most part, Baby Boomers have set the rules for today's work expectations. When Generation X(ers) emerged on the scene, they challenged the Baby Boomers and Builders but simply did not have the numbers to shape the workplace the way they would have preferred it.

Every generation experiences shared sense-making. It is a process in which individuals jointly interpret their environment and create collective accounts or narratives from which they derive meaning from organizational events. It moves individual perceptions and feelings to the state of group knowledge. Another aspect of group process is emotional contagion. Members of a group influence the emotions and behavior of other group members through the conscious or unconscious induction of emotional states and behavioral attitudes.

As each age cohort's self-identity is strengthened, it makes comparisons of itself to other generations. Social comparison exaggerates the difference between groups (Baby Boomer/Millennial) but strengthens in-group similarity and cohesion. As individuals find similarity within the group and compare themselves favorably to members of other groups, group cohesion and group identity are strengthened. A good example of this is how managers are experiencing Millennials in the workplace. There is a coherent, if not unified, voice about what Millennials are like and a constant favorable comparison of themselves to the Millennials.

WHO GETS TO DO THE SENSE-MAKING AND SET THE RULES?

Which generation is more apt to use the term "decorum"? Decorum is defined as good manners or correctness. All four generations in the workplace have an idea of what is correct—three have come to consensus. We argue that much of the generational tension in the workforce is due to the Millennials' desire to make their mark or imbue their values in the workplace. Okay, now we are back to "Doesn't every generation want to make an impact?" Yes! But, who gets to set the rules or make change?

One social concept that helps explain generational conflict in the workplace is *age norm theory*. Age norms are the ages viewed as standard or typical for a given role or status by the modal (dominant) group within a social system. There are several conceptions of norms, but most have three things in common:

Expectation

Expectation exists when there is a statement that specifies what response or behavior is expected in certain situations (what people ought to do).

Sanction

Sanction refers to the punishment of or disregard for people who violate an expectation (sometimes a sanction can be a reward).

A Group

Finally, group refers to a social contract in which "a group" of people are aware of and believe in the social norm and punish or sanction those who deviate from the norm.

When we look at the formal age structure (i.e., those who are older are in charge), power resides with older cohorts who share ideals about work attitudes, values, and behaviors. It can be argued that the larger the cohort (or group), the greater the influence over norms and expectations. We believe that generational tension in the workplace is most acute when there is a renegotiation of expectation. According to the National Center for Health Statistics, 83 million people were born between 1977 and 1997 (Millennial Cohort). Approximately 80 million Baby Boomers were born between 1946 and 1964 (Baby Boomer Cohort). GenX (38 million) is not a big enough group to challenge Baby Boomers, and even when the majority of Baby Boomers finally retire, GenX will still be outnumbered by Millennials. Despite Baby Boomers opting to stay at work a little longer, Millennials will outnumber both them and

GenX within 10 years. Millennials may not use the word "decorum" but they certainly will be helping to shape it.

It is important to note that sometimes violating group norms can result in reward or affirmation. For instance, an American teenager who enters college at age 16 is held in high esteem even though her advancement is not normal. In the same respect, skydiving is not an age-appropriate activity for a 94-year-old, but we admire and applaud such antics. In our opinion, many of the Millennials who are promoted into management get the invite because they appear different from their peers—more mature. They take an interest in their superiors and are able to reach up and make a connection. Therefore, they draw the attention and favor of the older generations. We found that approximately one in five Millennials take the initiative to connect with their superiors.

It is interesting that many refuse to acknowledge the idea that age cohorts can have distinct values and beliefs from one another. Critics are dismissive of the notion of *difference* and espouse the dangers of over-generalizing cohort distinctiveness. Ironically, their argument in itself is a generalization . . . "We all are the same and want the same things." Studies like ours allow for a healthy pause and reflection on what is *really* happening.

CHAPTER

3

THE EFFECTIVE MANAGERS VERSUS THE CHALLENGED MANAGERS

Our research design called on the human resource department of each organization in our study to provide us with three managers who were considered to be effective at managing Millennials and three managers who were perceived to struggle with managing Millennials. We conducted one-on-one interviews with each participant and then facilitated a focus group among the six managers.

We were surprised to learn that both populations (the effective and the challenged) perceived the Millennials similarly. Words like "entitled," "brash," and "smart" were common in all of the interview transcripts. The focus groups produced no discord or strong disagreement between the groups. Both the effective and challenged managers shared frustrations and experiences that aligned. Many of the participants left their interviews commenting that the experience was therapeutic for them.

If both populations of managers perceived Millennial employees the same way and had similar experiences with them, then what differentiated the good from the challenged? We begin by reporting what *did not* differentiate the managers. As we stated in Chapter 1, many believe that parenting has shifted from a focus on training to nurturing. One of our early hypotheses was that women would be better at managing Millennials than men. However, our data did not support such a notion. We also thought that managers who were parents of Millennials would be better at managing them in the workplace, another misconception we had to let go.

Our sample did not have a sufficient number of Millennials who were managers to adequately compare them to our data set, so we cannot say whether they are better at managing their own age cohort than managers who are older. That being said, Millennials who are managers generally score well on our Generational Rapport Inventory (see Chapter 14). In the same way that Baby Boomers and GenX(ers) understand each other, Millennials *get* Millennials.

One artifact that stood out among the managers who were considered to be good at managing Millennial employees was that most of them had served as a volunteer in a youth organization (Little League, AYSO, YMCA, Boys and Girls Club, Scouting, church youth group). One grocery store manager talked about how much he learned as president of the local little league. Many of the kids he had met through that experience ended up working in his store during their high school and college years. We identified two critically important characteristics required of anyone who volunteers to work with young people: (1) the ability to initiate a relationship, and (2) the patience to set expectations according to where the young person is, not where you want him or her to be. Both skills can easily be transferred to the workplace.

As we continued to sift our data, we found that the single most important differentiator between the effective managers and those who were challenged is that the effective managers exhibited the ability to suspend the bias of their own experience. In other words, they started with the Millennial's experience and not their own. Some of our challenged managers would say, "What experience? They have no experience!" If someone cannot suspend the bias of his or her own experience, that person will insist that "the way I did it" is the blueprint for everyone else. The inability to suspend the bias of one's own experience will inhibit self-reflection or learning. For instance, "Why am I so bothered by the fact that my employee wants work-life balance?" "What threats do Millennial values represent?" More importantly, "How will I need to change?" One manager we spoke to claimed to have lost three marriages and favor with his children because of his work ethic. He resented his Millennials for prioritizing family and friends over work. Obviously, his projection onto the Millennials kept him from facing his own "stuff."

Simply put, failing to suspend the bias of one's own experience excuses managerial leaders from the adaptive work that is required of them to manage in today's world. Part of the adaptive process is getting outside of the orbit of your own experience and entering the world in which Millennials live.

An underlying premise of this book is that the people with the most responsibility have to adapt first. It may sound cliché, but by setting an example, managers will create an environment in which the less mature will adapt. Adapting does not mean acquiescing to the whims of an individual or a generation. Adaptive managers have the ability to create environments that allow for enough discomfort so that people will feel the need to change but safe enough so that they can change. We think that generational rapport is critical to creating such an environment.

MIND-SET

Perspective or mind-set is critical to performance. We discovered six areas in which the effective and challenged manager perspectives significantly differed (see Figure 3.1).

Perspective	The Effective Managers	The Challenged Managers
Adaptability	Talked about their own need to change to manage in "today's world"	Talked about how others needed to change to make it in the "real world"
Self-Efficacy	Believed there was something they could do about the situation	Believed that there was little they could do about the situation
Confidence	Allowed their subordinates to challenge them (ideas, processes, ways of doing things)	Sanctioned or punished their subordinates for challenging them
Power	Used the power of relationship versus the power of their position	Felt the only power they had was their positional authority
Energy	Working with twentysomethings made them feel younger	Working with twentysomethings made them feel older
Success	Saw themselves as key to the twentysomethings' success	Saw the twentysomethings as an impediment to their own success

Figure 3.1 The Different Mind-Sets Between Effective and Challenged Managers

Adaptability

The effective managers in our study considered the challenge of managing Millennials a personal growth opportunity. Although frustrated or even puzzled, these managers constantly referred to themselves as needing to learn and enhance their own management skills. The challenged managers talked about how their subordinates just needed to grow up and face the real world. Although there is some validity in such a perspective, the focus of their frustration was projected onto what others needed to do not on their own personal development.

Self-Efficacy

We explain the juxtaposed outlook by noting that the effective managers had an internal locus of control. That is to say they believed they could do something about their dilemma. Consequently, the effective managers were more optimistic about their future and the potential of their Millennial employees. On the other hand, the challenged managers exhibited an external locus of control. They viewed the Millennial challenge as something that happened to them and they were powerless to do anything about it. They believed themselves to be victims of circumstance. It is not that they did not want to be good at managing Millennials, they just did not know where to start or what to do.

Confidence

The effective managers talked about allowing their subordinates to challenge them. At times, the managers even provoked a challenge if they did not perceive follower commitment or understanding. They spoke of making the effort to be a better listener, allow for debate, and being open to embracing the ideas of others. The challenged managers were threatened when questioned by their subordinates. They sanctioned noncompliant followers. They used their power to adversely impact scheduling, time off, and opportunities for promotion of employees who questioned them.

Power

Another clear difference between the two groups of managers was how they viewed their position and authority. When the challenged managers experienced relational tension they defaulted to using the only thing they had—their positional authority. Overuse of positional power usually manifests itself in declarative statements like, "I am the boss" or "I have been doing this since before you were born." If you find yourself spending more time proving yourself rather than expressing yourself, you may be relying too heavily on your positional power. When faced with relational tension the effective managers opted for relational power and used positional authority as a last resort. They considered empathy as being key to building trust with Millennial employees. One manager said, "If they know you care about them, they will go to hell and back for you!"

Energy

One of the more common phrases we heard from the effective managers was, "Working with them makes me feel younger." They spoke of being energized by the optimism, creativity, and raw enthusiasm Millennials bring to the workplace. The effective managers talked about the high value Millennials place on work being fun. Obviously, productivity and protocol were important to the effective managers, but they did not see anything wrong with embracing the emphasis on fun. Take an interest in what they are interested in but do not try to be a twentysomething. They do not expect to be the best of friends, they just want you to be friendly. Conversely, the challenged managers lamented about how the Millennials made them feel older. They particularly do not like what Millennials listen to, what they wear, or what they did over the weekend. In fairness, many of the challenged managers were trained to not fraternize with their subordinates. One manager said, "I was taught not to build a relationship with a subordinate because you may have to fire 'em someday." It is what we call *self-protecting* behavior. It is difficult, if not impossible, to build trust without a relationship.

Success

Perhaps the most telling differentiator between the effective and challenged managers was that the challenged managers considered Millennials to be an impediment to their own personal success. One manager commented, "I am a very good manager and I have always gotten along well with others, but *they* make me look bad." Another said, "I don't understand them; I just don't hire anyone under age 30." The effective managers viewed themselves as being key to the Millennials' success. They referred to personifying roles like mentoring, counseling, advocating, sponsoring, and teaching. Their success was linked to the success of the Millennials they worked with.

FOLLOWING UP WITH HR

When we completed our analysis of the data collected, we were fascinated to discover that, with the exception of only a handful of managers, we agreed with the selections human resources (HR) made for both the effective and challenged groups. So we returned to our HR leaders and asked what criteria they had used for selecting the participants. We were told that the challenged managers struggled with turnover, complaints, absenteeism, communication, and low productivity. The effective managers did not. We asked HR leaders if they knew what differentiated the two groups. They could see the aforementioned negative outcomes, but they were not sure what precipitated those outcomes.

We want to reiterate that all of the participants in our study desired to be successful managers. Much of their job-related anxiety was tied to not knowing what to do about their frustration with the Millennials they managed. While being able to talk about it was helpful, simply seeing that others had similar experiences to theirs was not sufficient. Equipped with the competencies we identified in the good managers, it would not take much for many of the challenged managers to move into the effective group.

Our intention in the next few chapters is to move beyond generational finger-pointing to real solutions. We unveil what we learned from both the effective and the challenged managers. You are able to identify what you are doing right and what may be inhibiting or undermining your effectiveness. New behaviors can be learned but are difficult to sustain without the support of *right thinking*. Our hope is that you are compelled to examine your own thinking with respect to managing across generations.

You are now far enough into the book to realize that you as a managerial leader really are the main character. When we first started to research generational tension in the workplace we identified managerial leaders as key to the solution because they have the greatest amount of responsibility and influence with respect to daily duties and interactions. That, coupled with the well-established fact that employees leave managers and not organizations, we believe that equipping managerial leaders is the best way to address the challenge of integrating Millennials into the workforce.

In his bestseller *How*, Dov Seidman argues, "It is no longer *what* you do that sets you apart from others, but *how* you do what you do." The effective managers in our study showed us *how* to manage.

CHAPTER

4

THE POINTS OF TENSION BETWEEN MANAGERS AND MILLENNIALS

The Millennials are coming of age in unprecedented numbers. They are bringing with them both a facility and comfort with cutting-edge technologies—both communication and computing. This is creating the same kind of bewilderment that the parents of television-addicted Baby Boomers felt in the 1950s and 1960s. Each generation moves into the workforce, and eventually into positions of power and influence in society. The new generation then begins to make demands on the nation's various institutions to change. They push for accommodation to their beliefs and values. The larger the generation, the more clout it has. The Millennials, because of their sheer numbers, are in the process of making those demands on the United States in general, and on managers in particular. And the relationship of managers with Millennials is the focus of our study.

We have discovered that there is a fundamental disconnect between managers and Millennials. The disconnect has led to organizational tension, less-than-full engagement on the part of Millennials, and misdirected effort by managers. This has led to unforeseen frustrations making it almost impossible for managerial leaders to identify disconnects and discover solutions. When managers properly identify the points of tension, disconnects can be reframed as opportunities to connect and build trust rather than discord. This cannot be overstated. The power of this model is that it transforms points of tension into points of connection.

During our interviews, we were intrigued to find that both the good and challenged managers we spoke with experienced similar tensions in managing Millennials. While studying in more detail thousands of statements collected during interviews with both managers and Millennial employees, we recognized a pattern of responses that we refer to as *perceived orientations* of Millennials. We use the term "perceived" because the orientations are based on how managers reported their experience of working with Millennials. Perceptions are not necessarily reality, but perceptions acted on or unchecked often become reality.

We struggled over the terminology used to represent the data from our interviews. Many of the descriptive terms the managers in our study used could be considered negative or even pejorative. Some of the statements may even offend some readers. For that, we apologize in advance. We decided to stay true to the descriptions the managers used for one important reason. The tension is real. It is the reason we wrote this book. It is therefore essential that we preserve the fidelity of the comments we collected. We could not have made this point any better than one human resources vice president who warned us: "If you softened the edginess of those labels, I'd laugh you right out of my office and ask you who you've been talking to!"

Further, psychological integrity suggests that the credibility of our work requires that we preserve the emotions as they were expressed by our study participants.

In order to test the face value validity of our model, we asked hundreds of Millennial participants in our study for their reactions to the perceived orientations. Believe it or not, they agreed with the descriptions! We were just as surprised at the response as you will probably be. The reason Millennials can agree with these statements is because they recognize that the intrinsic values they hold cause their cohort to be perceived just as we described.

There is obviously more to the story than just the perceptions of those who work with Millennials. Understanding the behaviors behind the perceived orientations will help managers reduce tension and build trust within their teams. People's behaviors are driven by their beliefs and values. This is true for every generation. As we described in Chapter 2, every generation in the workplace today holds a distinct set of core values molded by events that shaped the world during their youth. Leaders who understand the values behind the behaviors that are perceived negatively by others have an edge in maximizing the potential of their workforce. The nine orientations of Millennials as experienced by our managers are: (1) autonomous, (2) entitled, (3) imaginative, (4) self-absorbed, (5) defensive, (6) abrasive, (7) myopic, (8) unfocused, and (9) indifferent. For every perceived orientation, we have listed a set of corollary intrinsic values. As you can see, intrinsic Millennial values are normal, if not admirable (see Figure 4.1).

Once we identified the perceptions managers had of working with Millennials, we listened to how the managers responded to each of the orientations. Our aim was to understand just what separated managers who were successful in working with Millennials from those who struggled. We discovered that successful managers practiced a set of core competencies that are essential to effectively managing Millennial employees. The competencies fall within three behavioral categories: (1) adapting, (2) communicating, and (3) envisioning.

Adapting is the willingness to accept that a Millennial employee does not have the same experiences, values, or frame of reference that you had when you were the same age. We refer to this

Perceived Orientation	Millennial Intrinsic Value	Required Managerial Competency
Autonomous	Work-Life Balance	Flexing
Entitled	Reward	Incenting
Imaginative	Self-Expression	Cultivating
Self-Absorbed	Attention	Engaging
Defensive	Achievement	Disarming
Abrasive	Informality	Self-Differentiating
Myopic	Simplicity	Broadening
Unfocused	Multitasking	Directing
Indifferent	Meaning	Motivating

Figure 4.1 Orientations, Intrinsic Values, and Competencies

as suspending the bias of your own experience. Adapting successfully may require adjustments to your management style. In some cases, it may require changes to your organization's policies and procedures. Several major corporations found that they were better able to remain true to their mission by making their policies more accommodating to the expressed values of Millennial employees. The adapting competencies are ''Flexing with the Autonomous,'' ''Incenting the Entitled,'' and ''Cultivating the Imaginative.''

Communicating refers to the ability to make a connection at a relational level. It is the primary area where tension can escalate into emotional conflict. In the saddest cases, professional relationships deteriorated so much that we observed personal attacks. For the manager who is committed to succeeding despite relational tension, communicating is essential. It is about staying engaged even when both parties are frustrated. The communicating competencies are ''Engaging the Self-Absorbed,'' ''Disarming the Defensive,'' and ''Self-Differentiating from the Abrasive.''

Envisioning is about lifting the horizons among the unmotivated and myopic. It incorporates management practices that create both meaning and accountability for the Millennial employee. In practice, envisioning entails connecting employees' personal goals and aspirations with the organization's objectives. Without the Adapting and Communicating skills, it is highly unlikely that envisioning can take place. The envisioning competencies are "Broadening the Myopic," "Directing the Unfocused," and "Motivating the Indifferent" (see Figure 4.2).

Perceived Orientations of Millennials	Generational Rapport Competencies
Autonomous	*Flexing*
Millennials express a desire to do what they want when they want, have the schedule they want, and not worry about someone micromanaging them. They don't feel that they should have to conform to office processes as long as they complete their work.	The ability to modify workplace expectations and behavior. It requires empathic listening and the willingness to adapt to different ways of doing things.
Entitled	*Incenting*
The attitude expressed in Millennials that they deserve to be recognized and rewarded. They want to move up the ladder quickly but not always on management's terms. They want a guarantee for their performance, not just the opportunity to perform.	Incenting involves recognizing the reward expectations of Millennials and designing a path that reconciles it with performance expectations. It requires identifying Millennial values and aligning recognition and reward with those values. It calls for informing employees about advancement opportunities and frequent appraisal of their development.
Imaginative	*Cultivating*
Millennials are recognized for having a great "imagination" and can offer a fresh perspective and unique insight into a myriad of situations. Their imagination can distract them from participating in an ordered or mechanistic process.	It is the ability to identify and encourage creativity in others. It requires the capacity to create and facilitate environments in which people can release their imagination at work and have fun.
Self-Absorbed	*Engaging*
Millennials are perceived to be primarily concerned with how they are treated rather than how they treat others. Tasks are seen as a means to their ends. Millennials are often preoccupied by their own personal need for trust, encouragement, and praise.	The ability to reach out and relationally connect with direct reports. It requires taking an interest in the employees as a person and finding points of connection.

Figure 4.2 Millennial Orientations and Managerial Competencies Defined

Defensive

Millennials often experience anger, guardedness, offense, resentment, and shift responsibility in response to critique and evaluation. They want to be told when they are doing well but not when they are doing poorly.

Disarming

A proactive response to conflict. It involves de-escalating intense interactions, listening, being fair, and embracing resistance.

Abrasive

Perhaps due to technology, Millennials' communications style can be experienced as curtness. They are perceived to be inattentive to social courtesies like knowing when to say "please" and "thank you." Whether intentionally or not, their behavior is interpreted as disrespectful or usurping authority.

Self-Differentiating

It is the ability to self-regulate and "not take personally" the comments, gestures, or actions of others. It is being aware of the "trigger" events that make you reactionary rather than responsive.

Myopic

Millennials struggle with cause and effect relationships. The struggle is perceived as a narrow-sightedness guided by internal interests without an understanding of how others and the organization are impacted.

Broadening

The ability to help Millennials connect the dots between everyday tasks and big picture objectives. Emphasis is placed on teaching employees how to recognize numerous options and potential consequences. It involves teaching organizational awareness.

Unfocused

Millennials, as a cohort, are recognized for their intellectual ability but are often perceived to struggle with a lack of attention to details. They have a hard time staying focused on tasks for which they have no interest.

Directing

The ability to clearly communicate what is expected. It entails avoiding ambiguity and not assuming you have been understood. It requires both questioning and listening to ascertain the employee's readiness level for a task or goal.

Indifferent

Millennials are perceived as careless, apathetic, or lacking commitment.

Motivating

The ability to inspire Millennials to find meaning in the everyday work they do and to see how their contribution matters.

Figure 4.2 Millennial Orientations and Managerial Competencies Defined
(*Continued*)

Obviously, mastering the nine competencies will help you to effectively manage an employee of any generation. However, the competencies are exponentially more important when managing Millennials. Builders, Baby Boomers, and GenX(ers) have been working long enough to "get" each other and therefore are more likely to understand where management is coming from even if they disagree. Millennials do not have enough experience to have developed that understanding yet.

THE CONSEQUENCE OF INEXPERIENCE

If you are a manager and still not convinced about the benefits to be gained from making the effort to engage your Millennial employees, then maybe this book is not for you. But we hope you stick with us a little longer. This section contains a truly remarkable discussion, one of tremendous optimism, energy, and willingness to engage on the part of Millennial workers today, despite a societal organization that favors seniority. We expect younger people to pay their dues. Many managers told us so, in just about those words. This is not lost on Millennial employees, as you will see on the next few pages. Even so, we encountered a keen understanding among Millennials of the value of—and an eagerness—to gain experience.

This story takes place in the context of ageism, discrimination against or sanctioning of individuals because of their age. As you might imagine, where Millennials are concerned, ageism is a multi-edged sword. We know, swords usually only have two edges, but we have found four kinds of age bias at work here, two of which work in favor of Millennial employees, and two against.

One common bias we all fall prey to is the tendency to assume that individuals we encounter, including people we may work with daily, exhibit all of the traits and behaviors generally associated with their age cohort. Age stereotypes (e.g., older people are resistant to new technology) depict older persons as being less than desirable employees, particularly for technically demanding jobs. Employers default to negative stereotypes when they have limited information about applicants and project onto individuals certain perceived group characteristics.[1]

Recently, the problem of age discrimination has received increased attention. Many experts suggest there are two reasons for the growing interest: (1) the high costs connected with early retirement, and (2) an increased proportion of older persons in the population. Although the concept of ageism or age discrimination has been around for decades, age prejudice is still considered socially acceptable. Recently more attention has been given to the subject. Sociologist Todd Nelson sees a correlation between Baby Boomers nearing or entering retirement age and an increase in academic and popular interest in aging.[2]

Ironically, it is the Baby Boomer phenomenon that stirred our interest in studying Millennials in the workplace. We were concerned with "who" was going to take the Baby Boomers' place in organizations and the "disconnect" that seemed to be emerging between the age cohorts.

Ageism is mostly applied to the "older" segment of the population, but we want to take a look at the other side of the age equation. We found it interesting that when managers compared Millennials favorably to other age cohorts, it had to do with their openness to change and try new things. Although one may stereotype older workers as slower, less willing to change, or less technologically sophisticated, we also believe that there are negative stereotypes that impact the career opportunities (pay scale, promotion, benefits, etc.) of Millennials.

We know it is challenging, if not bordering on the incredulous, to think of Millennials as being victims of ageism. After all, our culture worships youth. Spanish explorer Juan Ponce de León, Puerto Rico's first governor, was searching for the Fountain of Youth when he traveled to Florida in 1513. Today people carry Ponce's spirit of eternal youth as they pursue the promise of every hair tonic, wrinkle cream, exfoliate, and injectable procedure. Futurist marketing guru Faith Popcorn has written on the phenomena she coined as "down-aging." Popcorn says, "Down-aging is a redefining down what appropriate age-behavior is for your age . . . 40 is now what used to be 30, 50 is now what used to be 40, 65 is now the beginning of the second half of life."[3] Famed lyricist Bob Dylan—who turns 69 years old in 2010—offers a blessing of eternal youth in his 1962 hit "Forever Young."

You may be asking how someone can be marginalized when everybody wants what they have. One explanation could be *stereotype threat*. Stereotype threat is the threat of having the negative characteristics stereotypically associated with a group applied to a particular individual, whether justified or not. People only experience stereotype threat when a negative stereotype about their group is relevant to performance on a specific task.[4] For instance, left handed golfers are not as good at putting as right handed golfers. Individuals who are easily identified with a cohort may experience greater susceptibility to stereotype threat.[5] The perceived orientations of Millennials could adversely impact their job opportunities.

Many of the managerial leaders we interviewed resented having to adapt to the Millennials. We discovered that there are managers who even refuse to hire them. We suggest, therefore, that it is possible that Millennials can be marginalized. We mean so in the context of being prevented, in the short term, from experiencing meaningful participation in organizational life.

Negative stereotypes can adversely impact the willingness of a managerial leader to mentor or help a young person—particularly when the older employee sees the younger employee as an economic threat. Managerial leaders may also be put off by attitudes and behaviors that are not consistent with their own. Perhaps the most damaging sanction a managerial leader can deploy is to not engage the young employee or do so in a way that is condescending. Here lies the marginalization. When managerial leaders superimpose their own experience (cohort-related values) over the younger workers (i.e., they ought to be quiet in meetings for a certain period of time) and the younger workers act out of their own experience (cohort-related values), a sanction may be imposed in the form of negative feedback. Studies show that people who receive constant negative feedback often show lower levels of effort as a result.[6]

Negative feedback tends to lower self-efficacy (the belief in one's own ability to achieve successful levels of performance). A key indicator of one's future success is self-efficacy.[7] Managerial leaders can negatively impact a person's self-efficacy by misusing their position or power.

We wanted to explore the idea of reverse ageism to see if Millennials felt barriers to job opportunities as a result of their age. So we did a survey with college juniors and seniors who were student leaders at California State University Long Beach and Vanguard University of Southern California. The criteria for participation was having had worked at a job in which they reported directly to a manager.

The five survey questions are:

1. Have you ever felt that you were treated differently at work because of your age?

2. If so, in what ways have you been treated differently at work because of your age?

3. Do you perceive being a younger worker to be an advantage or disadvantage in the workplace? Please explain why you chose advantage or disadvantage.

4. When you think of your work experience, for which reason do you believe you would be denied opportunity for advancement? (Age, Gender, Race, Ethnicity, Religion)

5. Have you ever felt that an older worker intentionally gave you a hard time?

Q. Have You Ever Felt That You Were Treated Differently at Work Because of Your Age?

We discovered that 64.3 percent of the students felt that they were treated differently at work because of their age. When asked how they were treated differently, they articulated feelings of being condescended to or disregarded for their lack of experience. We have included a few verbatim comments:

> "I wasn't given as much responsibility as some of the other workers."

"I have been talked down to, not taken seriously, underestimated."

"I was treated like as if I don't have enough experience; like as if I do not know how to do certain tasks that are easy to figure out; like as if I'm not capable of taking on certain responsibilities that I feel adequate in accepting, etc."

"People treat you like you don't have much experience or much to offer."

"They wouldn't give me the harder tasks because they felt I wouldn't be as experienced."

"They thought that I was not as smart as them or was not capable of doing their tasks."

"I was treated differently because of the misconception that I didn't know what I was doing. However, that wasn't the case."

"People have spoken to me as if I was a young child with smaller words or with the tone of their voice."

"I felt like upper management felt I was incapable of performing more difficult tasks because I am younger than most of their employees."

"I was treated like I was mentally handicapped just because I was only 20 years old, compared to everyone else who was in their mid-thirties. They talked to me slowly and acted like I couldn't pick up anything new because I wouldn't understand it."

"I have been treated like I was a young child because of my age."

"I been given less projects, called names such as kiddo, tiger, etc."

"As a mortgage broker, it is very difficult to convey to customers that you are in fact capable of doing the job as well as someone older. But in such an important, and complex transaction, I understand it."

Q. Do You Perceive Being a Younger Worker to Be an Advantage or Disadvantage in the Workplace?

Although the majority of students felt that they were treated differently because of their age, 67.9 percent thought their age gave them an advantage. When we isolated the students who answered that they felt treated differently (question 2) and correlated them to believing they were advantaged or disadvantaged (question 4), 72.2 percent believed their age was an advantage in the workplace. When asked to explain their choice (question 5), those who considered their age to be an advantage fell into three categories: (1) we have more time, (2) we are more teachable, and (3) we are more relevant.

We Have More Time

"You have the ability to be with the company longer and learn new things."

"It really could go both ways, but for the most part it is an advantage because you have much more time than older workers."

"I have an opportunity to know what all of the older employees know, and I am only 19. By the time I am their age, I will have mastered that profession."

We Are More Teachable

"Because you have the opportunity to learn more and be more open to mistakes. An experienced veteran has to be able to be almost perfect with no mistakes and a lot more pressure."

"Since I'm young, I can pick up things more easily. I am easier to train and teach."

"I think being young should be seen as an advantage because we are fast learners, hard workers, and we are good at achieving our goals."

"Advantage because I can pick up on things more quickly and adapt to different work styles more easily."

"I think being younger is an advantage because I learn faster, adapt to change more easily, and am more eager to learn and participate."

"It is an advantage because younger workers are more ambitious and willing to learn. This allows for training of the employee to what the company needs."

We Are More Relevant

"Because I am in touch with the customer in a way many older employees cannot be."

"I have newer knowledge and am more technologically based."

"I think that companies are looking for younger creative minds as the business world is changing every day. Young people bring a breath of fresh air and new ideas."

"I choose advantage because employers tend to like young and enthusiastic workers."

"I think it can go either way, but I think it is more of an advantage because 'younger' is being perceived as somewhat more creative and innovative today."

"I see being younger as an advantage because I feel like managers like to work with younger inexperienced workers more than older workers. With older people, managers have to deal with a lot of opinions about how things should be done and a lot more expectations. I think that managers like to work with younger people because they are more in tune with trends and what is popular in society. I think managers are also eager to pass down their knowledge and experience to young people just starting out."

The fact that the students feel discriminated against, but still think they have an advantage, may explain why there is little interest in exploring if or how young people are discriminated against because of their age. Perhaps younger workers are more optimistic about the future because they have more time to overcome "age-related" discriminatory practices. Conversely, older workers who experience discrimination may exhibit pessimism about the future because they have less time to overcome age discrimination.

The students who considered being young a disadvantage could be categorized into two sentiments: (1) their lack of experience and (2) being looked down upon because of their age.

Lack of Experience

"I choose disadvantage because an older person usually has more experience than a younger person."

"I think employers like to hire people with experience and usually hire people that are a little bit more mature and older because they expect you to have less experience and not know how to be a good manager."

"You don't have as much experience."

Being Looked Down Upon

"Disadvantage, because they don't take younger people as serious."

"I think it's a disadvantage because people don't take you seriously when you're young. They think you have no experience and you don't know what you're doing."

"Well, I do believe that there are both ups and downs for each. I would say disadvantage because people do not give you the respect granted."

"People view you differently because of age."

Q. When You Think of Your Work Experience, for Which Reason Do You Believe You Would Be Denied Opportunity for Advancement? (Age, Gender, Race, Ethnicity, Religion)

More than 60 percent of the students viewed their age as being the reason for being denied opportunity for advancement. We are curious as to how 50-year-olds would answer the question. It would stand to reason that length of tenure in the work environment would provide opportunity for other forms of discrimination to be experienced. It is obvious that "age" discrimination is more acute at the beginning and twilight of one's work life.

Q. Have You Ever Felt That an Older Worker Intentionally Gave You a Hard Time?

Again, more than 60 percent of the students felt that they had intentionally been given a hard time because of their age. When we went back and looked at the verbatim comments, we noticed that much of the articulation was comparative, if not outright competitive. That is to say that there was an "us versus them" theme. As an example, "I have newer knowledge and am more technologically based." We recognized a similar theme when interviewing managerial leaders on the subject of how they were experiencing working with Millennials. "They believe they [Millennials] bring high value to the workplace but do not seem to recognize the incredible value older workers bring, like experience."

It is telling that in the 2008 Democratic Primary then-Senator Obama had the majority of the youth vote. His inexperience was not an issue to young voters. Rather than stretching his limited experience into something it was not, he focused on portraying himself as having good judgment. Another presidential hopeful took a different approach. Senator Clinton's strategy was to emphasize her experience. Later, when she began to lose ground in the race, she changed her campaign from talking "experience" to using words like "readiness."

In the student verbatim comments on the previous page, you can clearly see that managerial leaders and Millennials are perfect for one another–the experienced coupled with the learner. Ironically, one of the biggest roadblocks to successfully managing Millennials is perhaps a managerial leader's greatest asset—lived experience. It seems counterintuitive, but if you acknowledge the Millennial's experience before you reference your own, you will have a greater chance at successfully managing them.

Perhaps the most remarkable thing here is that in spite of negative feedback, and in the face of an organizing principal of society that withholds privilege from them, we found a heartening—albeit competitive—optimism about future opportunities to contribute in their professional capacities among the Millennials we surveyed. We think that any manager can tap into that capacity if he or she is willing to apply the techniques laid out in the chapters that follow.

Millennials, like any other generation, will have to make adjustments to assimilate into the workforce. But, we are suggesting that the people with the most maturity need to adapt first. Quite frankly, if you are waiting for Millennials to grow out of their values, you may risk missing the best of what they have to offer!

In the chapters that follow, we look at the nine orientations of Millennials as well as the nine competencies essential for leading this vibrant and ambitious cohort.

DISCOVER THE CORE COMPETENCIES NEEDED FOR MANAGING TODAY'S WORKFORCE

5

WHEN LETTING THEM HAVE IT THEIR WAY MAKES SENSE

Flexing with the Autonomous

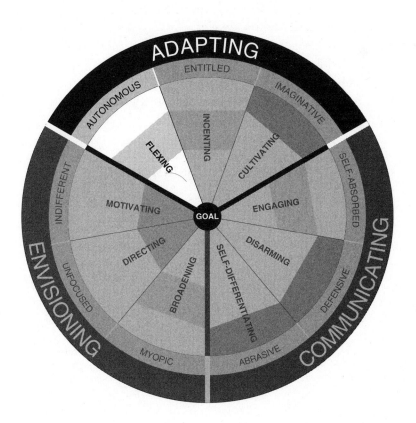

I kissed a lot of butts to get where I am today, and now it's time for someone to kiss mine.

—A Consulting Team Manager

I told them that I could only work three times a week, and they scheduled me five times a week . . . This has happened to me twice. So, I ended up quitting.

—A Millennial

We want to have a say about when we work and how we do our work.

—A Millennial

All things being equal, when there is a choice between getting your way and going their way, go their way. The idea that leaders and managers are going to change members of the current generation into what they want them to be is a strategy destined for failure. Only by flexing with the concerns of Millennials will today's managerial leaders have opportunity to develop the trust and rapport required to lead them.

THE MILLENNIAL INTRINSIC VALUE

Work-life balance is one of the most celebrated values of the Millennial generation. They work to live—not live to work. It does not mean that they are lazy. It does not mean that they do not want to work. They want work that is meaningful. They want

Flexing	Autonomous
The ability to modify workplace expectations and behavior. It requires empathetic listening and the willingness to adapt to different ways of doing things.	Millennials express a desire to do what they want when they want, have the schedule they want, and not worry about someone micromanaging them. They don't feel they should conform to office processes as long as they complete their work.

Figure 5.1 Flexing with the Autonomous

work that is challenging. And they want it on their terms. They want time for friends, family, and doing the things they enjoy. They do not necessarily wish to forego upward mobility or opportunity for advancement but at the same time they show little or no reluctance to change companies in an effort to have it all. The fact that many of them are relationally and materially untethered affords them the option of moving back home or cohabitating so they can hold out for the job they want—or the job that gives them what they want.

The Great Recession has spawned speculation that insecurity in the job market will curtail Millennials' free-agent attitude. We would not bank on it. Among the four generations in the workforce, Millennials have been the least impacted by the recession. Millennials will be investing in their pension as the stock market recovers and purchasing their first homes near the bottom of the market. They are optimistic about their future and they should be.

The intrinsic value of work-life balance leads to a workplace value that Millennials hold—*autonomy*, but not for the reasons you would think. They do not wish to be free of direction or supervision. Rather, giving Millennial employees autonomy on the job communicates that you believe in their ability and trust them. Like other employees, they detest being micromanaged. However, other generations dismiss a micromanager as anal or controlling. Not Millennials. They take micromanaging behavior personally because it connotes a lack of trust or confidence in them. A common refrain heard from Millennials in our study—though not in exactly these words—was, "Show us what you expect us to do, and then get out of our way."

THE BIAS OF EXPERIENCE

We can imagine you are thinking to yourself, "I have made sacrifices my whole career to get to where I am, and now you are telling me I need to be more flexible?" Yes, but only when it makes sense.

The lamenting manager we quoted previously may have been more frank than others. However, her sentiment was shared by many of the managers we interviewed. One of the unspoken promises of the workplace is that if you are hardworking and loyal then your day will come after years of patience—you will get to influence your organization the way previous generations of leaders did in their turn. Junior employees will feel obligated to listen to you. You might even get to call the shots outright. Many managers are finding that is not their experience. Quite frankly, there is an unrealized expectation that experience and position should count for something in the eyes of their subordinates. The expectation is there because managers remember their own journey of entering and assimilating into the workforce. We heard comparison after comparison, "I would have never asked for time off having only been on the job for a month." Or, "He told me he was a volunteer high school coach and needed to leave for practice by 2:30 PM every day; I'd love to have seen my old supervisor's face had I told him something like that." It wasn't that it was hard to say no to some requests, they just resented being put in the position to say no or to be the heavy.

As difficult as it is, you have to suspend the bias of your own experience and not compare yourself to them. It only creates frustration and resentment unless you are using yourself as the "bad" example (addressed in Chapter 9). A great exercise is to listen to yourself or your colleagues and make a note of when comparisons are being made. It happens more frequently than you think.

Another notable frustration managers experienced stems from the fact that their own effectiveness depends on what they perceive to be an undependable group of workers. They are undependable because there is no certainty they will be here tomorrow. A university vice president illustrates this sentiment:

I started here at $19,000 a year. The job is a big job. It requires a lot of work, but people stayed longer and there wasn't kind of this movement all over the *place. Now it just feels like—and not just here but with colleagues at other universities—it's hard for us to keep our staff at those lower levels for longer than a year or year and a half. And that, obviously, has an impact on the staff and on the office as a whole. It impacts our goals and how we accomplish those goals. It makes it hard to do work because you're constantly retraining people, and that takes a lot of time and energy. So when we go through job interviews, we ask each person: can they see themselves here for three years? We don't ask for a signed contract, but we do ask them up front. It's our hope that they would have the intent of staying here three years, and they all say "oh, yes absolutely." Then at a year, they're usually looking at other options, or even leaving at that point. I think giving your word means something, seems to mean something different now, and most of my staff see that with their Millennial staff they manage, that giving your word doesn't really mean much to most of them.*

The university vice president, though frustrated, eventually enumerated several good business arguments for flexing: realizing organizational goals, reducing training expenses, and maximizing time investment. We add a few more: employee recruiting, retention, and the transfer of tacit-knowledge.

One of the biggest challenges facing organizations over the next 10 years will be employee procurement. Lately, Wall Street, Detroit, and the medical industry have feared competition from the federal government but the real competition with the feds will be for young talent. Many organizations have wised-up and they are taking seriously the need to adapt their recruiting messages to the Millennials. One example is Xerox's employee recruiting campaign. The message is that you can be you at Xerox. Notice the subtlety in the online ad, not only can you be you but we affirm you (see Figure 5.2).

The test for companies will be to live up to their recruiting advertising. Sometimes marketing can get ahead of development and make the mistake of overpromising and under-delivering. Organizations may have the savvy to sell themselves as employers to attract Millennials. But will they have a management team that can keep them?

Figure 5.2 Xerox Employee Recruiting Advertisement
Source: http://www.xeroxcareers.com

PSYCHOLOGICAL CONTRACT

We believe that all of the nine competencies are critical to retention, but flexing in particular affords you the time to build rapport with employees. Flexing is also perceived as a good faith effort to meet Millennials where they are and a willingness to negotiate expectations. In essence, flexing is a visible expression of the *psychological contract.* Chris Argyris introduced the concept of a psychological contract to address the white space in the employer–employee relationship that does not get addressed by a formal, written contract. The function of the psychological contract is to reduce employee insecurity and build trust. The concept of a psychological contract is 50 years old, but never has it been more useful than for understanding what shapes the workplace behavior of Millennial employees. It explains the angst Millennials experience when deciding whether to stay or go. They weigh their obligations to the organization against the obligations of the organization to them. If they sense an imbalance in realized expectations, they do not protest. Why bother getting into an argument with an authority figure who can only tell you how things used to be when she was young when one can just leave? If you haven't noticed, Millennials have a pre-occupation with the obligations of management toward them. One manager said it perfectly, "It seems all I hear from them is, 'What have you done for me lately.'" Expectations are not static. We believe that flexing demonstrates a good faith effort on the part of managers to address the real-time expectations of Millennials. Flexing is the dynamic for an ongoing dialogue and negotiation of expectation. Willingness to be flexible with respect to scheduling, process, and expectations gives Millennials a feeling of influence on what happens to them in the organization.

A subtle yet powerful managerial adaptation in perspective is to understand that the best way to get your expectations across to Millennials is to start with what they expect of you. We have provided a diagram (Figure 5.3) for you to think about your expectations in relationship to those of Millennials.

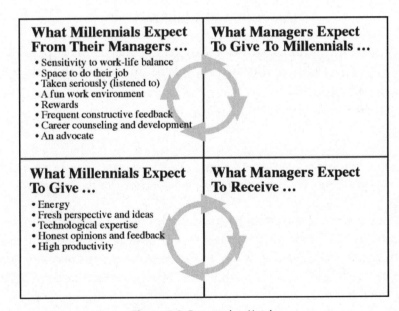

Figure 5.3 Expectation Matrix

LEARNING FROM OUR SUCCESS

A great example of flexing came from a golf pro we interviewed. He talked about working with Millennials, "They have so much going on, and I try to work with them so they can do things, but I also try to talk to them about their priorities." While willing to be flexible about scheduling, he also took the opportunity to communicate his expectations through helping them establish priorities.

A grocery store manager told us that empathizing and being fair was the key to working with Millennials. She talked about trying to understand what they were experiencing and how it affected their job performance. She also gave us new insight that, although there are areas or times in which a manager cannot be flexible, the manager can still build trust by not playing *favorites*. "They are looking for consistency from me. You don't always have to give them what they want but you do have to be fair."

LEARNING FROM OUR FAILURE

Contrast the good examples with another grocery store manager who insisted that it was the employee who must adapt to his leadership and, if they did not "get it," they'd have to go. He justified not hiring twentysomethings in the following way:

> They are transitory. They'll occupy the space with no intent of staying . . . their job just pays the bills. They are focused on what they want but don't see work as a way to get there. I don't want to hassle with the younger ones.

It was no surprise when he told us of his recruiting and retention problems. We can only wonder how many potentially valuable Millennial employees he passed over because of his unwillingness to be flexible. It is not that this person is necessarily a bad manager; rather it is that he has a generational blind spot that does not permit him to see twentysomethings in terms of their potential to do excellent work and become valuable assets to his organization.

Unfortunately for him (and for his employer), the result of his frustration is managerial paralysis. The manager cannot resolve his frustration with the autonomy orientation of the new workforce, and he is not open to the new approaches of working with them that would make his managerial efforts worthwhile. Unfortunately, this particular situation was not unique in our research. In fact, it was quite common.

BEST PRACTICE

One retail manager we interviewed developed an excellent solution to the problem of scheduling: He created a scheduling team—made up of regular employees—and empowered them to create and manage the store schedule. He just asked that they take ownership of the schedule and that they get each employee to sign-off on it. A headache became a leadership development opportunity and being a member of this team became a desirable position.

The outcomes were remarkable. All shifts were covered, and employees proactively protected the schedule and held one another accountable because they did not want to lose the autonomy they had gained. Also, the manager was able to build awareness and empathy among employees about the difficulties he faced in some managerial tasks, because the members of the scheduling team experienced the frustration of scheduling firsthand. Finally, the schedule became a symbol of the manager's flexibility. Of even greater significance to the employees, it also became a symbol of their empowerment.

The Transfer of Tacit Knowledge

Stop and think about it. Every organization on the face of the earth at one time or another is dependent on entry-level people. Arguably, the greatest competitive advantage an organization has is not in the knowledge that resides in its company manuals, but the knowledge that is captured within the experience of people who have spent a career acquiring it. Tacit knowledge can only be transferred through relationships. If there is a *disconnect* between the experienced and the young, odds are that tacit knowledge will not be retained in the organization.

In a Nutshell

There are two major concerns Millennials have when it comes to workplace satisfaction: (1) the freedom to negotiate their job description and (2) management's recognition that they have a life outside of work.

Some might suggest that being flexible with Millennials is an invitation to make managers a doormat for employee manipulation. We disagree. Having no boundaries and being a pushover for employee demands is not what flexing is about. Flexing is *not* giving in to whatever employees want to do at work. Flexing is the ongoing conversation between managers and Millennials about, "How can we do our best work together?"

Letting Millennials have it their way makes sense when . . .

They desire work-life balance

They desire a challenge

They want to find meaning in their work

They want to have a voice

They want to gain experience

Scenario

Trying to Hire for the Graveyard Shift

Sally is manager of a drug store in the San Francisco Bay Area. She is finding it increasingly difficult to hire for the midnight to 8 AM shift. She tells how many of her potential hires show

---

up for the interview looking "very different" with respect to how she would dress for an interview.

Because it is the graveyard shift, Sally decides to take a chance by hiring a young man who looked as if he were a young vampire. She instructed him that every employee is responsible for two merchandise aisles and the displays on each end. Part of each employee's responsibility entailed making sure the shelves were fully stocked, properly faced, and that appealing product displays adorned the end of each aisle.

After arriving to work on two consecutive mornings and seeing that her new hires' aisles had not been cared for properly, she was prepared to tell him to really get lost. That is, until she noticed his displays. They were the best in the store and professional looking. Most of her employees were not fond of having the responsibility for displays.

She thought she could either fire her new hire or take away the responsibility of aisle upkeep and give him charge for all of the displays in the store. The decision would be a departure from how she was trained to manage the store. But on the other hand, she could possibly salvage one employee and make many other employees happy at the same time.

Q. What should Sally do? What are some risks related to changing store policy to salvage her new hire? What are some upsides to making the change?

CHAPTER

6

REWARDING THE RIGHT THINGS IN THE RIGHT WAYS

Incenting the Entitled

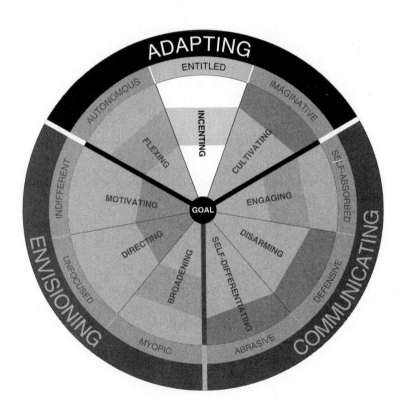

They played soccer as kids and they expect constant praise. They got a trophy just for showing up! And they expect the same at work.

—Fitness Facility Manager

Anything extra-nice I do, they act as if I owed it to them!

—Nonprofit Manager

I think being younger is a disadvantage because I feel those who hold managerial positions right now do not think highly of my generation. They think we are spoiled and are not hard workers, yet I think the opposite.

—A Millennial

Dealing with twentysomethings—many of whom embody the entitlement orientation—has been one of the most frequently mentioned issues with respect to leading and managing Millennials. There is something about an entitlement attitude that makes every manager bristle.

THE MILLENNIAL INTRINSIC VALUE

Millennials value being rewarded. Not unlike other generations, increase in pay, bonuses, and promotions are enthusiastically embraced. However, Millennials also value time off and the opportunity to participate in community or social responsibility projects during company time. They are not high on titles for

Incenting	Entitled
Incenting involves recognizing the reward expectations of Millennials and designing a path that reconciles it with performance expectations. It requires identifying Millennial values and aligning recognition and reward with those values. It calls for informing employees about advancement opportunities and frequent appraisal of their development.	The attitude expressed by Millennials that they deserve to be recognized and rewarded. They want to move up the ladder quickly but not always on management's terms. They want a guarantee for their performance, not just the opportunity to perform.

Figure 6.1 Incenting the Entitled

the sake of having a title or cookie-cutter employee of the month programs. It is safe to say that Millennials value what they value— not what you value! So before you try to reward them, be sure to ask them what they want. Millennials interpret reward and re-cognition as affirmation. Whether it is an actual trophy, or some-thing that creates positive memory, the important thing is that it connects twentysomethings and has symbolic value to them.

THE BIAS OF EXPERIENCE

When it comes to the *entitled* orientation, managers cannot help but compare themselves to Millennials. There is a perception among the managers that they did much more for far less when they were entering the workforce. Many commented, "We just didn't have the expectations Millennials do or, if we did, we would never verbalize them."

A storyline from HBO's *Inside the NFL*[1] sparked sharp opinion from former National Football League players, Dan Marino, Cris Carter, and Cris Collinsworth as they talked about the differences between today's players and those of the era in which they had competed. The story was about a wide receiver who played for the Minnesota Vikings. The player's grandmother died and he took nine days off to attend the funeral and to tend to his grief. The absence caused him to miss one game. The team fined him one game's paycheck but the player's council (made up of teammates) approached the team management and advocated for their col-league. As a result, management rescinded the fine.

Cris Collinsworth started the conversation, "Is this league in such a new school place now that we wouldn't even recognize it if we went back to play? What is a player's council? I know what it was when I was playing; we went to Roy Rogers for lunch and complained about Forrest Gregg [his coach], but we would never tell him." Dan Marino chimed, "It was a dictatorship. Whatever Don Shula said, that was it." Needless to say, the idea of a player's council was not only a foreign concept to them it was a symbol of something going wrong. It was interesting that their responses to the subject matter did not begin with the player in question but with their own experience, particularly with their relationship to authority, "We were afraid of our coaches." Later in the dialogue Cris Carter offers, "I don't believe the younger players have a love for the game." He talked about his own experience having had his own grandmother die when he was a player. He only took one day off for the funeral and did not miss a game. His coach (Buddy Ryan) even chewed him out for having a bad game. Each of the former players agreed that they would not have taken a game off, because it would have been looked at unfavorably by their respective coaches and they did not want to let their teammates down.

Whatever you think about the conversation, it is a great example of how we compare our own experiences favorably to those of others and use the comparisons as a means for expectation or judgment.

Perhaps you remember the SNL sketch *Grumpy Old Man* played by Dana Carvey. He opens the bit with, "I'm old and I'm not happy. Everything today is improved and I don't like it!"

We think you would agree that there is nothing wrong with having expectations. The stress you have has to do with perceived unrealistic expectations on the part of the Millennials. Pandering to twentysomethings' wants without regard for their performance, and offering rewards without desired outcomes, ultimately undermines both their development and your effectiveness. The challenge is rewarding the right things in the right ways.

Here are three keys to incenting Millennials: (1) create incentives that twentysomethings value, (2) clearly and thoroughly state desired outcomes and expectations, and (3) provide timely and fair assessment of their performance.

REWARDING THE RIGHT WAY

Some incentive programs are destined for failure because they ignore the participation or values of the recipient in the design process. Such attempts are referred to as need-based programs because they depend solely on management guessing correctly what the employee needs or wants. Sometimes they work but more often than not, they do not work. One Millennial who worked as a trainer at a fitness facility told us, "One of my favorite customers asked me where the nominating forms for the 'Company Star of the Month' were. I told him I would break his neck [edited for de-emphasis] if he submitted my name." The trainer went on to tell us that none of the employees wanted to be the *Star of the Month*, "All you get is your picture on a plaque and a parking spot that is about the same distance from the building as every other spot. I am a fitness trainer. I don't mind walking." What do you think he would have preferred?

Victor Vroom wondered the same thing. Reward had to be more than just guesswork. He suggested that people are motivated by how much they want something and how likely they think they are to get it. As a result of his study, he developed *expectancy theory*. There are three components to his theory: (1) *Expectancy* is the belief that a particular level of effort will lead to a particular level of performance; (2) *Instrumentality* is the expectation that successful performance of the task will lead to the desired outcome; and (3) *Valence* is the value an employee assigns to the possible reward.

One of our clients, a Fortune 500 company, had secured a large contract that had delivery date incentives built in that were quite lucrative. The senior plant manager cast a compelling vision for the project, the sacrifices required, and the payoff that awaited the company. Employees responded by going from two to three shifts and maximizing their efforts. The project was delivered on time and under budget. The company earned the contract bonus. The employees were elated and in addition to the overtime they had earned, anticipated a generous reward from their company. A celebration meeting was planned and all employees were invited. Employees eagerly awaited the news of their bonus but discovered the sum of their reward was balloons, cookies, and punch on the plant floor. In dismay, one disappointed worker upset the cookie table and uttered "I don't want your *!$& cookies." Although our example is extreme, it illustrates the concept of valence. If employees do not value the reward, management will not get the effort or productivity it desires. Sometimes management even gets the opposite.

REWARDING THE RIGHT THINGS

Even if you get the recognition and reward right, *incenting* still can be a frustrating process for both management and employees. Communicating how one gets recognition and reward can be challenging. In some cases, managers throw up their hands and project their distress onto the Millennials by saying, "They don't appreciate anything. I don't even know why I try" or "Anything nice I do for them, they just expect it." On the other hand, Millennials say, "Management just tells us stuff to get us to do things, but when we do them, management just says we're not ready."

One very important *aha* we experienced in our interviewing process was that Millennials interpret incentives as guarantees. Illustrated in Figure 6.2 is the difference between what manager's *say* and what Millennials *hear*.

What Managers Say . . .	What Millennials Hear . . .
If you take the transfer, it is the right step toward promotion.	If you take the transfer, you will be promoted.
If you get up to 100 case files, we will revisit you becoming a junior partner.	If you get near 100 cases, you will make junior partner.
If you do good work, turn in all of your assignments, and attend class regularly you should get an A.	If you turn in all of your assignments and attend class, you will get an A.
If you finish handpicking the golf balls on the driving range, we will talk about you getting off work early.	When you finish handpicking most of the golf balls on the driving range, you can leave.

Figure 6.2 The Difference between What Managers Say and What Millennials Hear

One explanation for what Millennials *hear* is referred to as *selective perception.*[2] It happens when listeners unintentionally filter out some parts of the intended message because it contradicts their beliefs or desires. The more sensitive the communication is, the greater the chance of *selective perception.*

KEEPING THEM INFORMED

Successful communication results when the person sending the message and the person receiving the message have a shared understanding of the message. Trust can easily be eroded if there is ambiguity with respect to objectives and expectations. One thing we learned over and over is that Millennials hate ambiguity (see Chapter 12). The importance of clear communication was stressed by one of the managers:

> *If you think you have communicated what the expectations are and the rewards that will accompany those being met frequently enough, you haven't! They need to hear these things three to four times more often than we think they do. So I have a reminder on my desk that I see every morning that says "Catch your employees doing well and tell them so!"*

If you feel that you are not being heard, one easy adaptation is to consider communicating in the medium that your younger workers prefer. If someone drops in on you, drop in on him. If someone calls you, call back. If someone e-mails, e-mail back. If someone texts you . . . you get the idea.

Keeping them informed means having an ongoing dialogue about what they want, what you believe they need to do, and their progress.

LEARNING FROM OUR SUCCESS

One manager said that the best way to incent Millennials is to give them the space to try different tasks:

I give my staff the opportunity to do some of the things that maybe would enhance their job and that they would enjoy. I think people get restless much more quickly today. They want to be promoted and they've been here a year and "I deserve this" and "I deserve that." There definitely is a sense of entitlement. I try to set their expectations early on. A lot of it is just continually talking with them. I can't tell you how many times I have heard "I've been here four years and I should be promoted by now." But without the recognition that we do your job evaluation every year and here are the things you need to work on. When we don't see growth in those areas, why would we promote you just because you've been here four years? We don't say it like that, obviously.

The key is that she manages the expectations of the Millennial with concrete objectives that are communicated frequently, clearly, and evaluated in a way that is constructive.

One manager, the owner of a golf supply store, reported to us that he was unhappy with his twentysomething employees. They would just stand around the store socializing when they were not helping customers, as if their time was their own. He was frustrated with their lack of attention to detail, "I don't want to have to tell them to straighten the merchandise, clean the counters, and stuff like that." He began to attribute their behavior to character. We suggested that his employees needed to know what he expected of them, the reason why he expected such behavior, and how they would be rewarded for their performance. At first he was resistant, exclaiming "They should already know this, and isn't a paycheck enough?"

Rather than write off the employees, the manager decided to take our advice. He stressed the fact that customers expected a neat and clean environment in which to shop. He explained that by keeping the store clean and using their nonbusy times to fix displays, restock, and straighten up the store, they were helping him to manage overtime costs. Next, he set aside a portion of the store's profits to be used for year-end bonuses, and created a monthly appreciation where he would recognize and reward excellent work by taking them out golfing. He still has to remind the employees to do the "little things" he wants done around the store, which continues to frustrate him, but the manager reports that his frustration level is much lower and that his twentysomething employees are putting in a sincere effort to meet his expectations.

The key to this manager's incenting approach is that he applied both incremental *and* long-term rewards tied to things his Millennials valued. He made every effort to make incentives unique, memorable, and tailored to the personalities of his twentysomething employees. The result is that his employees work harder for him, and he is happier with their performance.

There are many different ways to incentivize employee motivation. In their book *The Management Bible*, Bob Nelson and Peter Economy suggest that employees are most highly motivated when their managers provide them with:[3]

- Praise—personal, written, electronic, and public

- Support and involvement

- Autonomy and authority

- Flexible working hours

- Learning and development opportunities

- Manager availability and time

IN A NUTSHELL

It can be energizing, if not fun, to pull Millennials into the design aspect of incentive programs. It is one way to know that you are incenting the right way. Another valid reason is, "People tend to support what they help to create."[4]

The entitlement attitude can be successfully addressed in three ways: (1) creating incentives that Millennials value, (2) clearly and thoroughly stating expected outcomes, and (3) constructively assessing developmental progress on a regular basis.

Scenario

That's Just Not Our Philosophy

Libby is the managing partner of a large international law firm. Her firm recruits the best and brightest out of the nation's top law schools. Over the past few years, the firm has started to be concerned about their partner pipeline.

Since anyone in the firm can remember, the younger attorneys were assigned six-month to one-year assignments overseas. It was their way of paying dues and getting on the partnership track. Partnership was the tried and true golden carrot that could motivate in virtually any situation.

Recently, the younger attorneys have been turning down overseas assignments and even leaving the firm when pressured to do so. Libby is feeling the pain of seeing high potentials walk out the door and is trying to convince the other partners that the "old model" may be in jeopardy.

She suggested that the partners consider other ways younger attorneys can make partner. Her colleagues replied, "Our philosophy has worked for 50 years and we are not about to change now."

Q. Is Libby's thinking right? Is the partners' philosophy worth challenging? What incentives other than partnership may be useful for retaining talent? If you were Libby, how would you argue for change?

CHAPTER

7

THEY ARE AT THE HEAD OF THE CREATIVE CLASS

Cultivating the Imaginative

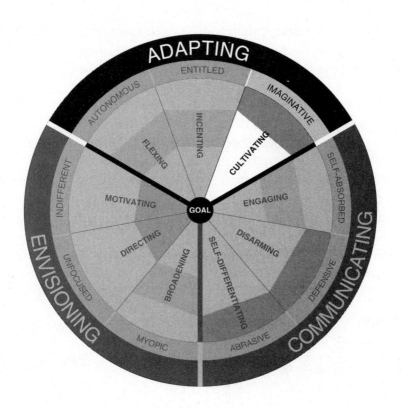

Isn't there an unspoken rule that you have to be here a couple of years before you can talk in a meeting?

—Planning Department Manager

You have to listen to them and not shoot down their ideas. We need to value them and their input. They are the front line who deals with the customer every day.

—Bank Manager

I think that companies are looking for younger creative minds as the business world is changing every day. Young people bring a breath of fresh air and new ideas.

—A Millennial

Tapping into Millennial creativity and the energy that accompanies it can be both incredibly satisfying and productive. According to many of the managers in our study, it can even make you feel younger!

THE MILLENNIAL INTRINSIC VALUE

Millennials value self-expression. They have both a desire and a need to make their mark on the world. They enthusiastically embrace change and thrive on brainstorming, creating, and problem solving. They have high expectations of themselves and the organizations in which they will work. One of our Millennial managers expressed it best, "I don't like just being at a job and

Cultivating	Imaginative
It is the ability to identify and encourage creativity in others. It requires the capacity to create and facilitate environments in which people can release their imagination at work and have fun.	Millennials are recognized for having a great "imagination" and can offer a fresh perspective and unique insight into a myriad of solutions. Their imagination can distract them from participating in an ordered or mechanistic process.

Figure 7.1 Cultivating the Imaginative

if I'm doing a good job, that's great, but if I come into a job that's running well, and it continues to just run well under me, I'm not happy. It needs to be like wow—I am making a difference. It's not so much that I want my name on it; I just want to feel like I made an improvement somewhere."

THE BIAS OF EXPERIENCE

In some instances, bad decisions can be the result of an over-dependence on experience. Neuroscience is demystifying how good managers can make poor decisions. Our brains are hardwired with two processes for decision making—(1) pattern recognition and (2) emotional tagging. Pattern recognition allows us to analyze a situation and emotional tagging tells us whether to react or ignore the information. Experience is the software the brain uses to recognize patterns. If you have done something long enough, your capacity to be able to anticipate and make quick decisions increases.[1] An obvious danger resulting from the bias of experience is getting stuck into one pattern of thinking—when we get stuck, we suffer from a regression of the imagination. That is to say that we cannot see things differently than they are presently or how they have always been. Even the most experienced and seasoned people can suffer from an over-dependence on their own experience. Another danger bias introduces is when emotional tags cloud judgment or overrule proper analysis.

Peter Gruber, director of the movie *Gorillas in the Mist*, tells of the nightmare of shooting on location in Rwanda with 200 animals that wouldn't "act." The screenplay called for the gorillas to do what was written and when they did not, the only option was to fall back on a flawed formula that had failed before—that of using dwarfs in gorilla suits on a sound stage. It was during an emergency meeting that a young intern asked, "What if you let the gorillas write the story? What if you sent a really good cinematographer into the jungle with a ton of film to shoot the gorillas? Then you could write a story around what the gorillas did on the film." Everyone laughed and wondered what the intern was doing in a meeting with experienced filmmakers. But ultimately they did exactly what she suggested, and the cinematographer "came back with phenomenal footage that practically wrote the story for us." Gruber says, "We shot the film for $20 million, half of the original budget." The moral: The woman's inexperience enabled her to see opportunities where others saw problems.[2] Gruber's experience did not allow him to think of filming before scripting, and his emotional tagging almost caused him to dismiss a great idea.

CREATIVITY AND COMPETITIVE ADVANTAGE

Companies often equate innovation and creativity with competitive advantage. Scores of articles and books have been written about how to spark creativity and innovation in the workplace. The mantra of "thinking outside of the box" has become somewhat cliché-ish, but the idea of suspending what "has been" in order to explore what "could be" will always be prescient. Peter Gruber's intern illustrated the clear advantage Millennials can have over the most seasoned of experts; she was not encumbered by her expertise or experience, and she was not afraid to pipe-in even though uninvited. Managers intuitively understand this, and that is why creativity and willingness to change are the two areas in which managers consistently compare Millennials favorably to other age cohorts. When it comes to creativity and using one's imagination, Millennials are plug-n-play. They are already outside of the box. The challenge is to not let them get bored or lose their energy.

As you well know, creativity doesn't generally fit a mechanistic or efficiency model. Many managers struggle with cultivating the imagination of Millennials because they manage job descriptions rather than people.

It is not surprising that many of the managers we interviewed described leading Millennials as equivalent to cat herding. The energy Millennials bring to organizations is sometimes experienced as distracting, but we find that most of the leaders we interviewed really do not want to suppress their energy and imagination. One manager playfully commented, "Just when you get one focused and engaged in a task, four more are floating off into 'who knows what?' They're all over the place. Usually it's fun, but sometimes it is just incredibly trying. I wonder sometimes if they forgot to take their meds on those days, or if this is just normal for them!"

MANAGERIAL BEST PRACTICES

Creative people benefit from being allotted chunks of time for focused thought and problem solving. They need time un-interrupted by the intrusion of organizational policies and mundane routines. If you give them the room they need, you will generally be impressed.

Anticipate Their Boredom

Many of the managers we interviewed talked about how quickly Millennials get bored with doing the same thing over and over. One of the many "ahas" we learned from our good managers was the notion of anticipating boredom. When their direct reports started to suffer from a lack of challenge, they were ready with a new test for their creative skills.

Don't Ask Them Their Opinion If You Are Not Serious about Hearing It

Millennials have not been around long enough to learn the un-spoken rules of meetings. If asked for their opinion, they weigh in with conviction and without reservation. The old school manager said, "If I wanted your opinion, I would give it to you." Many of today's managers know that the right thing to do is ask for feedback even when they don't *really* want to hear it. Their thought process goes somewhat like this, "I am asking for your opinion, but I hope you understand that I am only asking. Therefore I am not really wanting or expecting a response." One manager we spoke to shared his frustration with staff meetings, "Sure I invite opinions, but there is a protocol for participation. But it just seems that they [Millennials] don't really hold off what they're thinking. They're going to say what they're thinking, and it can come across very arrogant. In my generation, we earned the right to be heard. You know? So pay your dues, and then we're going to listen to what you have to say."

One of the quickest ways to turn Millennials off is to invite their participation and not really mean it. You are better off being autocratic than faking collaboration.

LET THEM KNOW WHAT HAPPENED WITH THEIR IDEAS

Millennials have a preoccupation with feedback, especially positive feedback. Their desire to make a contribution causes them to doggedly track the life of their suggestions and ideas. They want to know that they are taken seriously, if their ideas are being implemented, and if not, why.

One manager told us about inviting his team into a hiring decision. He formed a small ad hoc committee that met a few times to discuss what it was looking for in its search. When the manager settled on the lead candidate for the job, two of his team members became upset. They felt their advice was ignored, and more importantly, they saw the choice as a signal that the manager was taking the organization in a direction they did not think it should go. One of the disappointed team members resigned and left the organization. The other stayed but is reluctant to give energy to activities outside of his primary responsibility. Some may read of this manager's plight and say, "no good deed goes unpunished." In our opinion, his invitation to engage his team members in the hiring process was an excellent strategy. Early in the process, information was plentiful and thoroughly discussed among the team members, but the closer he got to the final decision, he relied more on his gut and had difficulty communicating what he was thinking and feeling. The manager's reluctance to communicate was interpreted as shutting the team out of the final decision. In the end, he became defensive about his decision and said his team was just going to have to deal with it. Here is a great example of doing something right, but because each of the players had a different understanding of the process and expectations for their involvement, it backfired. Here are a few things to consider when inviting Millennials to the table:

- Clearly state the process for decision making

- Ask them what they expect to receive for participating

- Communicate what you expect from them

- Use "what if" scenarios . . .

  - What if I don't take your advice?

  - What if I make a decision you do not like?

- When you are close to a decision increase communication

- Always have a debriefing meeting to discuss the decision that was made

  - Identify the contribution of each team member

  - Ask them what they learned from the process

  - Tell them what you learned from the process

  - Explain how you came to a final decision

LET THEM HAVE FUN

A study was conducted on creative groups of people and the function foolishness plays in their genius. Listen to a description of their behavior:

They get silly. They may suddenly decide to take an afternoon off for a picnic. They may play some light-hearted game on company time. They may decide to redecorate their workspace in weird, wild ways. Every now and then, they may break into uncontrolled laughter. They may put together a spontaneous party when they need to come down off of a high, or when they have worked extremely hard for an especially long time, or when they have made a breakthrough or hit a wall. They are prone to short bouts of ridiculous behavior.[3]

Jean Lipman-Bluman and Harold Leavitt explain the function that foolishness plays:

1. The escape into off-the-wall fun and games is thinking time. Temporary playfulness among adults clears the air, so they can begin to see the world in new ways. It disinhibits.

2. It is a way of moving toward deeper, easier, and more uncensored communication.

3. It's a relief valve, reducing the tensions imposed by the pressures of intense consuming work.

IN A NUTSHELL

Millennials may not have a lot of experience, but sometimes that can work better for you when it comes to creativity. Realize that Millennials are going to get bored so be prepared with a new challenge. If you do not seriously want their input, do not ask for it. Let them know what you think about their ideas. Let them have fun. It serves an important function for allowing the imagination to work.

Management Scenario

If an Idea Falls in a Meeting and No One Wants to Hear It, Does It Make a Sound?

Ryan was excited about his new job working for a business-networking firm. One of his responsibilities was to facilitate table discussion during monthly luncheons that focused on management and business development topics. The discussion usually followed a presentation made by someone who had a particular expertise on the topic of focus.

Ryan had interned at the company during his senior year of college, but had only been on the job for about a month, when he decided to suggest his boss change the format of the luncheons. He proposed that it might be good to sometimes have the table discussion before the presentation. His thinking was that the discussion was sometimes limited to the speaker's expertise rather than tapping into the expertise of the people around the table. Ryan's manager suggested Ryan put in a few years before trying to tell him how to do his job.

Q. Why would Ryan propose a new practice after his first month on the job? Was it appropriate? Why? Why not? If you were Ryan's supervisor, how would you handle his proposal?

8

FIRST THEM, THEN YOU

Engaging the Self-Absorbed

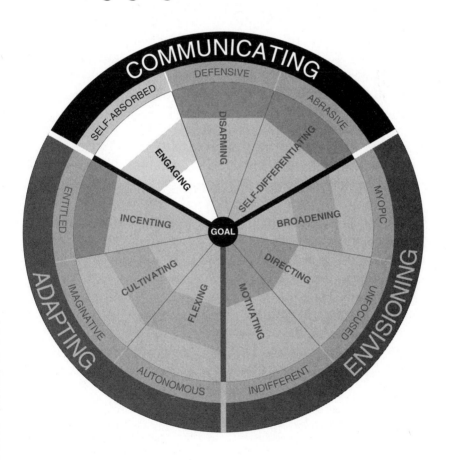

When I was coming up through the ranks, I reached out to my boss. I didn't expect my boss to reach out to me.

—Engineering Firm Manager

If I wanted to be a camp counselor, I would have gone to work for the Y.

—Syndicated News Program Manager

If they took the time to get to know us, I think they would like us.

—A Millennial

You have heard the story about two people having a conversation at a cocktail party . . . Mike asks Jim how he's been lately. Jim goes on and on about his new promotion, his golf game, his kids' recent achievements, and his health. Finally, Jim says, "We have been talking about me all night. Let's talk about you. So Mike, what do you think about me?" There are a lot of managers out there that feel like Mike.

THE MILLENNIAL INTRINSIC VALUE

Similar to the Baby Boomers, the Millennials' sheer numbers demand an audience. Millennials are used to getting a lot of positive attention and they like it. Not only do they like the attention, they expect it. When they enter work life, they anticipate the same consideration they have enjoyed at home, in school, and on the playing field. They want managers who will tend to their

Engaging	Self-Absorbed
The ability to reach out and relationally connect with Millennials direct reports. It requires taking an interest in the employee as a person and finding points of connection.	A primary concern for how one is treated rather than for how one treats others. Tasks are seen as a means to "my" ends. Millennials have a preoccupation with a need for trust, encouragement, and praise.

Figure 8.1 Engaging the Self-Absorbed

career development and act as an advocate for them. When faced with an adult who they perceive is not for them, they don't know what to do. That is why in many cases they turn to mom and dad for help with professors and managers.

One explanation for Millennial preoccupation with positive attention is the result of a subtle shift in parenting style. We believe there has been a swing from *training* to *nurturing*. That is not to say their parents (mostly Baby Boomers) did not emphasize training—they just placed a greater emphasis on nurturing. Many of the managers we interviewed told us that they perceived themselves to be more nurturing as parents than they remembered their parents being. It was not uncommon for a manager to share that he or she had never heard the words "I love you" from the lips of a parent. They knew they were loved; it just wasn't spoken. In keeping with age cohort theory, we looked for social markers that may have contributed to the shift in parenting styles. We encountered an unlikely source while touring the Museum at Bethel Woods in Bethel, New York. There it was, in a museum devoted to Woodstock and the 1960s, a section featuring Dr. Benjamin Spock. The tribute was recognition of Dr. Spock having penned the parenting handbook for a new generation of parents:

> Spock's ideas have become such a part and parcel of the parenting landscape that it's easy to forget how revolutionary they were. In post-war America, parents were in awe of doctors and other childcare professionals; Spock assured them that parents were the true experts on their own children. They had been told that picking up infants when they cried would only spoil them; Spock countered that cuddling babies and bestowing affection on children would only make them happier and more secure. Instead of adhering to strict, one-size-fits-all dictates on everything from discipline to toilet training, Spock urged parents to be flexible and see their children as individuals.
>
> Perhaps most revolutionary of all, he suggested that parenting could be fun, that mothers and fathers could actually enjoy their children and steer a course in which their own needs and wishes also were met. All this and much

more, including a wealth of helpful medical advice, was delivered in a friendly, reassuring, and common-sense manner completely at odds with the cold authoritarianism favored by most other parenting books of the time.[1]

It is quite remarkable how Dr. Spock's emphasis on being friends with your children, being flexible in your parenting style, having fun with your kids, and bestowing affection on them aligns with many Millennial intrinsic values.

The increased positive attention from parents is a good thing. However, managers need to be aware of how Millennials have experienced the primary authority figures in their lives. If you wish to engage them, it will be through a relationship that provides positive attention and affirmation.

THE BIAS OF EXPERIENCE

"Nobody asked me what I wanted out of the job when I was first entering the workforce. They just told me what was expected of me, and if I couldn't do it, they would get someone who could," one manager boasted. A reorienting of focus is occurring in real time for today's managers, from attention to what the organization expects of the employee to what the employee expects of the organization and the manager. Although it adds a layer of complexity to management's job, the real frustration is the preoccupation that Millennials have with their own experience without an appreciation for management's objectives.

A few GenX managers in one of our focus groups remembered wanting things to be different but having to adjust her own expectations, "If you think about it, we have a lot of similar values, but we [GenX] were willing to change, and what frustrates us is that they don't think they have to."

When you boil it down, Millennials expect special attention because they believe they are special. Their parents have told them, their schools have told them, television has told them. Now it's management's turn.

BEST PRACTICES

You have probably already recognized that many of the competencies work in tandem. The *Engaging* competency is somewhat of a baseline because it must be done well before one can master some of the other competencies. Fortunately it is one of the easier competencies to master.

One begins by shifting the focus from her or his own experience to that of the other person. As usually is the case with any kind of skill, those who do it well seem to do it effortlessly. The managers in our study who were best at engaging, told us:

> Sometimes you have to get to know each one of them. They're all different. And to me, I like try to relate to each one of them, and I try to remember what it was like when I was that age and how I thought.
>
> They have a lot of stuff going on. I don't mind them confiding in me. I feel good if I can help them out in any way. I'll just talk to them and ask them what is going on and usually they will talk to me about what they're interested in.
>
> I just try to relate to them because I have been there before.

The following chapter sections give our distillation of the thoughts, feelings, and practices that these "naturals" relayed to us. What our natural engagers told us, in essence, was: be empathic ("Got Empathy?"), "Get Closer, Be Curious," and "Grow Them." They also gave us a list of "don'ts": "Try to Like Them, Not Be Like Them," rethink some of the rules you were taught ("Rethink What You Have Been Taught"), and watch out for "Peer Pressure" and "The Fine Line."

Got Empathy?

The managers quoted above genuinely cared for their employees and how they were experiencing both work and personal life. Empathy is sensing another person's feelings and perspectives and taking an active interest in the others' concerns. It is what enables managers to have relational awareness. Would you rather work for someone who cares about you or someone who doesn't?

Get Closer

Relax, we mean in proximity. One manager told us that he felt that he had lost touch with the younger generation in his office so he re-engaged his employees by doing their job with them. Periodically, he would join his employees and work alongside them. The manager and his team would set small goals for the morning and he would buy pizza for lunch if they hit their target. Although his idea is not new, it makes sense. Relationships that develop at work often emerge simply due to proximity. One way to engage your Millennials is to work *next to* them.

Be Curious

It is no secret that Millennials are used to attention. They are not shy when it comes to talking about themselves, their ideas, or their interests. One of the best pieces of advice we heard was from a manager who told us: "I try to stay curious about them." The manager told of having read the book *Turning to One Another* by Margret Wheatley. The intent of Wheatley's book is to encourage people to have conversations that are important to them and the people they care about. Wheatley says:

> *Stay curious about each other. When we begin a conversation with this humility, it helps us to be interested in who's there. Curiosity is a great help to good conversation. It's easier for us to tell our story, to share our dreams and fears, when we feel others are genuinely curious about us. Curiosity helps us discard our mask and let down our guard. It creates a spaciousness that is rare in other interactions. It takes time to create this space, but as we feel it growing, we speak more truthfully, and the conversation moves into what is real.[2]*

Effective managers make it a point to have conversations with their employees. They stressed the importance of routinely making time to socialize with employees at work. They were also prepared for occasions on which employees came to them with problems—work-related or not. The key is to recognize that much more than casual conversation is going on. Trust is being built.

Grow Them

Those who are successful at engaging their Millennial subordinates experienced a deep sense of personal fulfillment when their employees became successful in their own activities. We encountered this many times over the course of our research. A health club manager in her early fifties, who seemed to have a knack for leading Millennials, describes what she most enjoyed about working with Millennial employees:

> *It is energizing to see them grow, to see their excitement about improving and their movement from the baseline.*

She invested in relationships, but she was more than a buddy or friend. In our interviews with her, we discovered that she created an exciting work environment. More than that, she wrote personal accountability plans for her employees. She developed a baseline agreement with each employee so that each one could track his or her own success. As a result of the trust built with them, she informally mentored many of her employees by helping them deal with personal issues—and to achieve goals—both within and beyond the workplace. Many of her employees told us that she was the best boss for whom they had ever worked.

SO WHAT ARE SOME BARRIERS TO ENGAGING?

In the next few paragraphs, you will discover a few misconceptions managers have about their efforts to relationally connect with Millennials.

Try to Like Them, Not Be Like Them

One mistake managers admitted to making while attempting to engage Millennial employees was by dressing similarly, talking like them, and listening to their music. News flash: that cool new spiderweb tattoo you have been thinking about getting on the back of your neck is not going to make you a better manager. (If you already have one, it is okay because that is really who you are, we hope.) Like everyone else, Millennials appreciate authenticity. But unlike you, they expect diversity almost to the point of taking it for granted. They do not expect everyone to be like them, and if you are a Boomer or GenX(er), Millennials really do not expect you to dress as they do or listen to the same kind of music. What they want is for you to be who you are, and for you to like them.

Rethink What You Have Been Taught

Perhaps the greatest barrier to engaging is a result of traditional *management training.* Many of today's managers were taught by their managers not to build relationships with their employees. Engaging is the area we get the most push back during our seminars and coaching sessions. Here are some of the arguments we hear from our clients and seminar participants:

- I was taught not to get close to them, because I may have to fire them someday.

- I don't think it is wise to fraternize and become drinking buddies with them.

- Familiarity breeds contempt, and sooner or later, they will use something against me.

- You have to keep clear lines between staff and management or else they will get confused.

- HR won't let me hang out with them, they say it is too risky.

We are not suggesting that you become "BFFs" (that is "best friends forever" in younger-generation speak). The successful managers in our study made a connection with their Millennial employees simply by taking an interest in them. That does not mean you have to become drinking buddies with your employees, hang out with them after work, or attend their family reunions. Nor do you get to stop worrying about the difficulties inherent in firing an employee who is unable or unwilling to fulfill his or her job responsibilities. But discipline "up to and including termination" will come up far less frequently with employees who are appropriately engaged, and you will spend far less time working with human resources to "work out" employees who are not "working out."

Peer Pressure

Even some of the effective managers were very careful in how they talked about relating to their employees. It was almost as if they thought they were doing something wrong. Listen to this manager:

I'm relational and nonrelational. I know for me it's important that I know my boss and feel like there's some connection there. And I feel like that's important for my employees. I meet individually with my team on a regular basis. I think it's important to know people that work for you, but we can't all sit around every day and talk about the night before. But I do think it's important to have some personal knowledge of your staff. I think that when there is a relationship, there is more of a sense of commitment and loyalty to you and to the organization. There is more motivation to get the job done. There is more of a feeling like you want to please somebody. So, for me, I feel like it's very important to build relationship with my team.

Later in the interview, we discovered that this manager was known to take her staff to movies in the afternoon and even entertain them in her home. She was highly relational. So why did she want to be perceived as nonrelational, too? First, because being nonrelational is equated with productivity in many work contexts.

The cultural environment in many organizations causes peer pressure among managers to work against constructive engagement. We found, for example, one company where a night manager who allowed the employees on her shift to make their own schedules was labeled a "pushover." It is surprising to us that organizations are not leveraging the strengths of some talented managers to make the whole management team stronger. We asked an all-star at managing Millennials if all managers in her company used the same guidelines. Reluctantly she admitted, "Sometimes you can see managers do things that you know are going to result in a mess, but we kind of stay out of each other's way and use our own styles." It is ironic that managers who engage their employees are sensitive to being perceived as too relational, while their counterparts show little concern over being perceived that they are not relational enough.

The Fine Line

We are not suggesting that engaging Millennial employees comes without challenge and frustration. Some managers felt that they had been taken advantage of because of their effort to connect relationally. They talked about the fine line between being liked and being respected, "Most of us want to be liked, but sometimes you can't be too buddy-buddy with them because you have to make sure that things stay on the respect level."

A manager who had recently opened her own tavern, but had almost no management experience, talked about learning how to be tougher, "I do know that I care and that's what they like about me. But then again that is why they tend to take advantage of me. I wonder sometimes when they call in and say they can't come to work if they would do that with a boss that was more business-like and firm."

If you are good at building rapport with your Millennial employees, do not let *peer pressure* or the *fine line* stop you from using what is a managerial strength for you. Play to your competencies. We really cannot emphasize that enough. Use the competencies where you are already strong to build up your strength in other areas. If you do feel run over or taken advantage of, some of the other competencies can help you. For instance, *Directing* is about setting boundaries for Millennial behavior and *Broadening* is about helping them understand how their behavior impacts the entire system, including you. *Self-differentiating* helps you to not take their behavior personally.

SOMETHING TO THINK ABOUT

Tom Rath, in his book *Vital Friends*, gives a startling statistic, "Employees who have a close friendship with their manager are more than 2.5 times as likely to be satisfied with their job." In the same Gallup study, 8 million people responded to the statement, "My supervisor, or someone at work, seems to care about me as a person." The people who agreed with the statement are more likely to stay with the organization, are more engaged with customers, and are more productive.[3]

A study by the Saratoga Institute found that the quality of relationship a worker has with her or his immediate supervisor accounts for 50 percent of job satisfaction.[4] There are many challenges that managers do not have control over in the work-place. Perhaps you used to think that one of those challenges was relating to the emerging workforce. Take heart, it is within your control and there is something you can do about it.

In a Nutshell

The more often that Millennial employees perceived their managers to be interested in them and in their personal devel-opment, the harder they worked for their managers. First them, then you!

Management Scenario

Why Can't We Be Friends?

During an interview with a couple of managers in our study, two distinct schools of thought emerged about being friendly with your direct reports. Heather suggested that it was unprofessional and dangerous to befriend direct reports. Her thinking was that someday she may have to fire or lay that person off, and it would just make it more difficult if they were friends. She also argued that a manager could be accused of playing favorites or be subject to criticism from other managers.

Heather shared a story about how she had confided in a subordinate and that subordinate used the information against her. As a result, she told us, "I am nice to them, and they know I will help them with work-related stuff, but I am not interested in being their friend."

Conversely, the other manager (Ron) talked about how important it was for him to connect relationally with his direct reports, "I think my greatest management skill is just taking an interest in their lives."

He considers it an honor that they confide in him and let him into their world. He even joked about feeling like a counselor. Ron agrees that boundaries are important. He didn't consider being drinking buddies or socializing outside of work as the only context for friendship. He also mentioned being burned due to befriending a direct report but felt that the upside far outweighed the downside. Ron said, "I spend the majority of my waking hours in this place, and I want to mean something to my direct reports, and I want them to know they mean something to me."

Q. Both managers make valid points. Is there a difference in their definitions of friendship? Which one do you think would be more effective cross-generationally? Why?

CHAPTER

9

FRAGILE, HANDLE WITH CARE

Disarming the Defensive

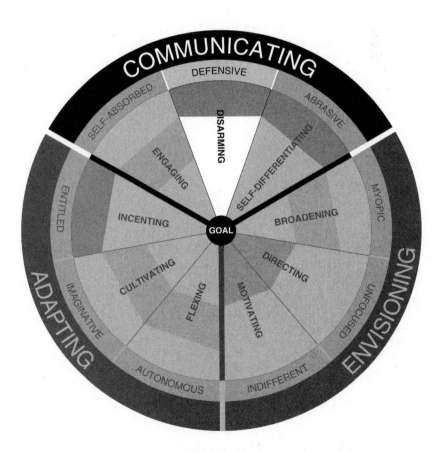

It is never their fault. And why not, I mean they've been told that they are special every day of their life while growing up, and then they come to work, and we say there's a problem and guess what, it's you! So what do we expect, of course they are going to be offended? It's just that you can't say anything to them without it blowing up.

—Shoe Company Manager

Sometimes I avoid giving feedback that is not positive because I don't want to deal with the drama.

—Real Estate Office Manager

They kind of deflect critique. I just roll with the punches and guide them in the right direction. Normally it takes a couple of confrontations to get through to them, but you have to be patient.

—Country Club Manager

We don't expect them to be our best friends, but when they critique us, we want them to do it in a friendly way.

—A Millennial

Constant affirmation has undermined genuine recognition and left too many members of the Millennial generation without the sense of security required to tolerate criticism or even listen to it.

THE MILLENNIAL INTRINSIC VALUE

Achievement is the intrinsic value that drives the Millennials' need to be affirmed. Feedback that is not interpreted as being affirming

Disarming	Defensive
A proactive response to conflict. It involves de-escalating intense interactions, listening, being fair, and embracing resistance.	Millennials often experience anger, guardedness, offense, resentment, and shift responsibility in response to critiques and evaluation. They want to be told when they are doing well, but not when they are doing poorly.

Figure 9.1 Disarming the Defensive

is met with anything from incredulity to counterattack—not only by them, but sometimes by their parents as well. In an article published in *FastCompany*,[1] Danielle Sacks gives an extreme example of a situation that would have been considered unthinkable less than a generation ago.

A 22-year-old pharmaceutical employee learned that he was not getting the promotion he had been eyeing. His boss told him he needed to work on his weaknesses first.

The Harvard grad had excelled at everything he had ever done, so he was crushed by the news. He told his parents about the performance review, and they were convinced there was some misunderstanding, some way they could fix it because they had been able to fix everything before.

His mother called the human resources (HR) department the next day. Seventeen times. She left increasingly frustrated messages: "You're purposely ignoring us"; "you fudged the evaluation"; "you have it in for my son." She demanded a mediation session with her son, his boss, and HR—and got it. At one point, the 22-year-old reprimanded the HR rep for being "rude to my mom."

This case illustrates the powerful new mix of defensive young employees and interventionist helicopter parents confronting managers today. It is no accident that these are hitting managers together in a one-two punch. There are many factors contributing to the defensive posture frequently encountered among Millennial employees. The most significant of these factors is the parenting style that became popular among Baby Boomer parents in the wake of Benjamin Spock's revolution. Though extreme, the example is not as uncommon as one might think. We interviewed more than one manager who received phone calls from parents who were not satisfied with their children's performance reviews.

Defensiveness manifests as taking offense, unwillingness to accept responsibility for one's actions, guardedness, resentment, and anger. In the workplace, these are often seen in response to criticism and evaluation. Even minor critiques have been reported to trigger loud and emotional outbursts.

The word "criticism" itself has become problematic in our language. The word's origin means "to analyze," but for many people—defensive or not—the word connotes a scathing attack. To a defensive individual, the *possibility* of criticism is especially threatening, even if the intent is constructive.

Millennials are under more pressure to succeed than their elders. They have been raised to excel at academics, sports, music, and their next *big hit* is work. They expect instant success, partly because the continuous stream of media content never shares with viewers the hard work that success actually requires. And they have been applauded and affirmed for every step they have taken. One of the authors recently was told "good job, Dad" by his toddler. At two and a half, she had heard it so frequently that it had become part of her vocabulary.

Modern affluence and ideas about child rearing might be creating a challenge for society through the mixed blessing of too much of a good thing. Parents have always wanted the best for their children. They want to make sure their children suffer no negative consequences, from the environment or their own actions. Economic prosperity allowed Boomer parents to indulge their protective and nurturing instincts to an extent not available to previous generations. Social commentators began to write about the helicopter parent last decade, though the phenomenon goes back further. Parents were seen hovering like helicopters, ready to get their "boots on the ground" the instant an intervention was required. They deploy themselves just as readily in response to threats against their children's self-esteem as to physical danger. When their children are in preschool, they monitor to make sure that all social interactions are smooth, for fear that the toddlers might develop a phobia against further socializing. In elementary school, they volunteer as "class parent" so they can be on hand to ensure that no situation is too stressful. At the same time, they push their children into as many after-school activities as possible in order to ensure maximal broadening, rounding, and nurturing. The practice of doling out awards to all participants is one of the results of the self-esteem movement. Needless to say, helicopter parents heaved a collective sigh of relief—

with a wink to one another—when each child received a trophy at the end of the season.

We should not be surprised to see parents experiencing difficulty in finally extricating themselves when their kids go to work, after having been actively involved in their children's lives, from infancy through college, and in many cases, graduate school. After all, unlike in prior generations, the children are not actually *leaving* to go to work. Young adult children are far more likely to live at home during their first few years after college than their parents were.

We're willing to bet that most readers will be "satisfied" if they can avoid having parents join the next performance review. This chapter is designed to help you disarm your defensive Millennial employees before mom or dad call HR. Seventeen times.

THE BIAS OF EXPERIENCE

Skeptical managers say, "What success? Their grades are inflated; they got a trophy just for showing up; and anyone can be an American Idol! They still have a lot to prove to me." Compare such sentiment to that of the Millennials in our survey who articulated feelings of being condescended to or disregarded for their lack of experience.

One of the more notable differences managers spoke about when comparing their experience to that of the Millennials was how their managers had reprimanded them. One manager put it rather colorfully, "They didn't care about our feelings or if we were going to quit. If you were lucky, they would shut the door, but people down the hall could still hear the 'butt chewing.'" Several managers we interviewed thought there was value in the unsentimental way they were handled early in their careers. They did not think they would have become successful without having had a manager or supervisor who was willing to get tough with them. From their current vantage, our interviewees felt that in their youth they lacked skills and judgment, and they also lacked the perspective to see it. The people they worked for had to rattle their cages in order to open their eyes. For many of the managers in our focus groups, the rough handling they received while coming up through the ranks was a badge of honor or rite of passage. We were treated to more color from a focus group partici-pant who summarized the changes this way: "Society as a whole is getting softer and gentler. Coaches' coaches are giving way to players' coaches. Drill sergeants are befriending recruits. Hell, even librarians won't tell someone to shut-up anymore."

None of the managers we spoke with expressed a desire to return to the days of over-the-top confrontations. It is worth pointing out that the "butt chewings," which were acceptable 20 years ago, are no longer considered appropriate. Those on each side of the generational divide have differing views of appropri-ateness in the workplace when it comes to politeness, expressing one's own feelings, and resolving conflicts. These differences even apply to subtle behaviors such as asking a superior why a task was assigned.

Keeping these distinctions in mind is particularly important when disarming a defensive employee. Studies suggest that people admire vulnerability in their leaders. Use yourself as a negative example, as illustrated in this fictitious quotation: "Your mistake pales in comparison to mine. I lost the company $20,000 because I signed a contract that we couldn't get out of. I should have read it more thoroughly." Talking about your own mistakes will help you to build trust with your Millennials. Not only trust, but also a greater confidence in your ability to lead. Even more important, employees (and their organizations) can learn by examining their failures in detail. A vice president we interviewed created a safe environment for hearing criticism by positioning herself as a learner, "It's a journey, and even though I'm your boss and a vice president, I don't know everything. I'm still learning and growing. Together as a team, let's take this next year, read through some books, and talk through what we want to be. We all have room to grow."

BEST PRACTICES

Before class one day, a Millennial who was an assistant manager at a surf and skate shop approached one of his friends who worked for him, "Dude, why didn't you show up for work yesterday?" Evidently the friend's response was not satisfactory to the young manager and so he continued, "We're friends, and we will always be friends, but if you ever hang me out like that again, I'll have to replace you. Now, where do you want to go for lunch?" The conversation took less than two minutes but it revealed volumes. In some ways, it violated convention—done in public and confrontational. But the result was remarkable evidenced by the friend's response, "You are right. I get it. I won't let you down again. How about Chipotle?" Here's what we learned from this remarkable young manager through this one encounter.

The Less Pomp and Circumstance, the Better

The confrontation was not dramatic—it was both informal and conversational. In Millennial speak, it means that the manager did not make a bigger deal out of it than need be. The more dramatic and formal the encounter (like in your office), the more you can expect anxiety and defensiveness.

Assure Them about Your Relationship with Them

The manager began the dialogue by assuring his friend about the state of their relationship. Whether the job worked out or not, the relationship was intact. Relationships are important to Millennials, as they are to people of every generation. But they have been taught to emphasize slightly different aspects of their relationships. They are accustomed to coaches, parents, and teachers reassuring them that the criticism about to be delivered in no way affects the esteem and warmth that is felt for them. They are more concerned with the state of the relationship than they are the consequence of their behavior. Assuring a Millennial subordinate of the value you place on your relationship with them will help him or her to accept unflattering feedback. The more you put them at ease relationally, the more open they are to critique. This is true with all people, but especially so in this multigenerational context.

Invite Them to Look Forward to Better Times

Asking his friend where he wanted to have lunch was an ingenious tactic used by our young manager. Not only did it affirm the status of their relationship, it was also an invitation to a more positive encounter.

LEARNING FROM SUCCESS

We have captured a few of the strategies that managers found to be very useful in helping Millennials keep their emotional balance so they could remain open to learning from their mistakes.

Suspend Snap Judgments

We invite you to try a simple exercise. Imagine yourself being asked the following question and then note the thoughts and feelings that arise in response: "Why do I have to make 250 copies"? Earlier we explained how our minds simplify decision making by use of pattern recognition and emotional tagging. In supervisory situations, the word "why" often alerts the listener to the possibility that his or her instructions are meeting resistance. Previous generations may have used "why" to signal defiance, but more often than not, Millennials really do want to know why. They have been encouraged to ask why at home, at school, and now they are asking why at work. How a person hears the word "why," and the subtext intended by the speaker, are generationally specific. So suspend snap judgments, embrace the "why," and even if you think it is resistance, embrace that, too!

Embrace Resistance

We have suggested that the points of tension experienced with Millennials can become places to connect. *Disarming the Defensive* is a great example of how to turn resistance into commitment. Gary Yukl argues that there are three possible responses to the influence of a managerial leader–commitment, compliance, and resistance.[2] Look at Figure 9.2. Where would you place *resistance* and *compliance*?

Many people place resistance at the opposite end from commitment. The reality is that resistance is closer to commitment than compliance. Resistance can be anywhere between compliance and commitment. It is common for lifelong friendships to have started with a conflict. Managers who accept compliance as a sign of commitment will find it difficult to develop others or to lead organizational change. Effective managers realize that resistance is better than compliance and embrace it. As one manager put it, "I really am one of those people that think rebellion every now and then is a good thing. I think it keeps things fresh and alive. That's really what I love." Resistance indicates dissatisfaction. Recognizing that allows a manager the opportunity to engage their Millennial employees by giving them the opportunity to voice their concerns.

Step to Their Side

If you meet resistance with opposite force, it will usually end up in a power play. A great example for going with resistance can be found in the Japanese martial art of Aikido. Morihei Ueshiba's goal

Commitment

Figure 9.2 The Commitment, Resistance, Compliance Continuum

was to create a martial art that practitioners could use to defend themselves while also protecting their attacker from injury. Aikido focuses not on punching or kicking opponents, but rather on using their own energy to gain control of them or to throw them away from you. One of the first moves in Aikido is to position yourself so that you see what your attacker sees. The goal is to move with her, not against her. When you encounter defensive Millennials, step to their side and try to see what they see and use their defensiveness as a means for connecting with them.

"Step to their side" is a phrase that negotiating expert William Ury uses in his work. Anybody who effectively manages Millennials knows that it takes negotiation skills. Ury's advice[3] is very applicable to managing Millennials when it comes to disarming defensiveness:

- Resist the temptation to argue

- Acknowledge their feelings, their point, their competence, and your differences

- Shift the encounter away from positional bargaining to joint problem solving

- Help them to save face

- Ask them for constructive criticism

- Reaffirm the relationship

- Aim for mutual satisfaction, not victory

Be Fair

"I think if you take the time to actually be a good listener, try to understand, and be fair with them, they will take constructive criticism," commented one of the managers in a focus group. Another manager challenged, "How do you determine what is constructive criticism and what is not?" The first manager responded, "I guess if you don't listen to their side of the story, you don't try to understand where they are coming from, and you are not perceived to be fair, then the criticism is not perceived to be constructive." She went on to tell a story of an employee who worked under a different manager in her store. The employee wanted to talk about his poor performance with her. She asked her colleague if it was okay before consenting to meet. The young employee started, "You know, I can't talk to him. I can talk to you. I have a lot of stuff going on at home . . . I'm not trying to do a bad job." She suggested that the three of them talk together and that maybe he should try and help his manager understand what was going on in his life. They met and it worked out. She reflected, "I feel good that I could help him out a little bit. I also got to explain to him what our job is, so he can better understand where we're coming from as managers. He's still here, he's happy, and he does his job much better now."

It takes time to "be fair" but it is not nearly as time-consuming as writing them up or having to replace them.

Learning from Our Failures

A company we were working with was experiencing high turnover. The positions were entry-level and labor intensive. The managers were exhausted with their young recruits quitting after only weeks on the job. Some of the managers blamed the turnover on the fact that Millennials could not be counted on. Others suggested they were not effective at finding the right Millennials. The employees who were quitting expressed that they were tired of being yelled at for problems that were not their fault, "I like the tips and the perks, but I can't handle being yelled at."

We asked management what issues they found themselves confronting the most and they replied, "It's all pretty much small stuff. Things they should know." One manager asked a couple of employees what could be done to make their jobs more tenable. Initially they were reluctant to answer candidly, but were eventually convinced of the manager's sincerity. "None of us feel like we have been trained properly. The people who trained us were leaving and they never got trained. We really don't know if we are doing things right or wrong. We get that you are busy with your job upstairs, but you don't know what it takes to do our job down here. We don't need someone yelling at us, we want someone who can show us what to do."

Nobody likes to be yelled at but Millennials are more frustrated by the fact that they are perceived to be bad employees. If you decide to ask for constructive criticism, be sure not to be defensive yourself. The worst thing you could do is to minimize their input.

They do not know how to fail because they were never allowed to fail. Over time, through failure, we learn to accept ourselves as real people. Until that happens, we are likely to try to preserve images of ourselves that are unrealistic. We cannot expect, however, that young people will choose to fail because they understand its pedagogical value. That tough job belongs to parents, teachers, and coaches.

The manager who gets hooked by excuses, the blame game, or a poor attitude will lose their balance and ability to disarm the defensive. In the next chapter, we talk more about the concept of getting emotionally hooked and what to do about it.

IN A NUTSHELL

Millennial employees' defensiveness is tied to their desire to achieve. If you correct them in a condescending way, they will not hear you. They respond to managers who care enough to listen to them, attempt to understand them, and assure them of the relationship. Once you have had to confront, be sure to invite them to look forward to their growth by regularly recognizing their progress, providing them with support, giving them constructive feedback, and showing them that you want them to succeed.

Scenario

Musical Booths

Anita, the director of an annual non-profit showcase that invites members of the community to learn about local services and volunteer opportunities, was stressing over the fact that she had a new administrative assistant. After helping Anita run the event successfully for several years, her former assistant took a similar position in another township.

The project was progressing on schedule, but Anita had a growing concern about her assistant's level of enthusiasm for the non-profit fair. Anita was having lunch with a trusted friend and couldn't help but bring up her concern in the conversation. Anita's friend asked her what she meant by "level of enthusiasm." She explained that the assistant seemed to be inattentive in some planning meetings and didn't give much input. Anita's friend offered, "You have been doing this for a long time, and I know you have a good system, but maybe your assistant doesn't feel like she has been given ownership of anything."

After returning from lunch, Anita asked her assistant if there was anything she would change about the upcoming event. Her assistant immediately responded and suggested that the layout of the booths could be improved. Her idea was to change the entire setup so that each booth could have better foot traffic and visibility. Though a huge change from previous fairs, Anita took the advice of her assistant and charged her with the execution of the re-arrangement. In the following weeks leading up to the event, Anita's assistant showed more energy and enthusiasm for the project.

The evening before the fair, the volunteer setup crew that had helped Anita for years showed up and saw the new booth arrangement. The supervisor of the setup crew told Anita

(continued)

(*continued*)

that the new schematic would take longer to construct and that it would create a foot traffic problem. He strongly advised that Anita go with the 'old way' of doing things, "Why fix it if it ain't broke?"

Anita struggled with the decision but decided to go with the old way of setting up the booths. When her assistant saw that the booths were being set up wrong, she approached Anita and asked, "What is going on?" Anita explained what the setup crew had said, and that it was a difficult decision, but she had to make it. Her assistant said, "You were going to do it *your way* all the time. Next time, don't bother to ask me what I think." She then stormed off to her car.

Q. Did Anita make the right decision? What would you have done? Now that the situation is to this point, how would you approach your assistant?

IT IS NOT ALWAYS ABOUT YOU

Self-Differentiating from the Abrasive

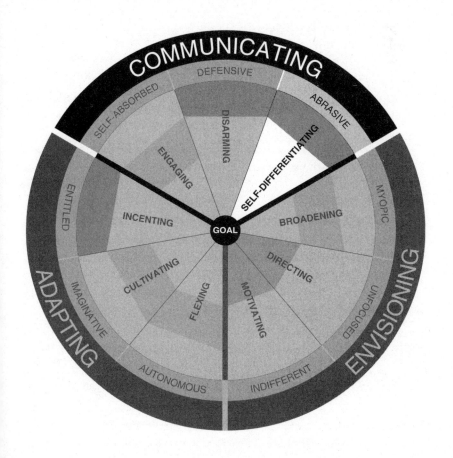

They assume it is okay to call me by my first name . . . like we are buddies—I am their boss!

—Hotel Manager

I found that it can be very difficult to take criticism from them. I've had to just let things go because it seems that they don't have a filter. They really don't hold off what they're thinking.

—Minister

I have been a people pleaser my whole life but I think they [Millennials] have cured me.

—Tavern Owner

I know it sounds harsh but why should I show them respect when they haven't earned mine?

—A Millennial

I believe one thing that often causes a rift between people in managerial positions and Millennials in the workplace is the lack of respect. The managers assume that we aren't informed or well educated, and that all we to do is play extreme sports and get piercings, when that is as far from the truth as they could possibly get.

—A Millennial

Unlike the other competencies, self-differentiating is something you do for yourself. It helps you to more effectively use the other competencies without getting emotionally hooked. It is

Self-Differentiating	Abrasive
It is the ability to self-regulate and "not take personally" the comments, gestures, or actions of others. It is being aware of the "trigger" events that make you reactionary rather than responsive.	Perhaps owing to technology, Millennials' communication style can be experienced as curtness. They are perceived to be inattentive to social courtesies like knowing when to say "please" and "thank you." Whether intentional or not, their behavior is interpreted as disrespectful or usurping authority.

Figure 10.1 Self-Differentiating from the Abrasive

especially important because poorly differentiated managerial leaders find it difficult to continue a relationship with people who disagree with them or who are not considered to be on their team.

THE MILLENNIAL INTRINSIC VALUE

Millennials value informality. It can be seen in the way they dress, talk, and negotiate organizational culture. Other generations understand the function of titles, but Millennials see them as perfunctory, if not an impediment to building real relationships. They believe calling someone by his or her first name is a sign of relational closeness and respect. By suspending formality, they expedite the more important relational exchanges.

Many of the Millennials we interviewed told us that the primary authority figures in their life are their most trusted friends. And who are those most trusted of friends? Drum roll, please. Their most trusted friends are . . . their *parents*! Consequently, they are most comfortable with authority figures when there is familiarity.

The Millennials did not invent informality—the Baby Boomers did. Most Builders still bristle at casual Fridays. Country clubs allow denim. Dinner clubs welcome the tie-less. The theater welcomes the coatless. Black tie events allow blue ties. The pastor of one of the United States' largest churches preaches in a Tommy Bahama shirt! GenX(ers) who make it to the executive level turn their office buildings into playgrounds. Informality is in.

THE BIAS OF EXPERIENCE

The familiarity that Millennials exercise is perceived by many managers to be a lack of respect for position and titles. A provost from one of the country's largest universities told us the story of a student who walked into her office unannounced and said, "Hello

Pam, we have to get together for lunch one of these days." The provost had mixed emotions, because on the one hand, she was happy that the student felt comfortable enough to stop by. On the other hand, she felt that the academy and her office are upheld by a certain level of institutional decorum. To simply call the provost by her first name and not "Dr." was a threat to her position and the institution. The provost decided not to take this lack of decorum personally. She realized there was more going on than a violation of protocol. This, she realized, was not an attack on her. She did not overreact to the situation, but instead, she adapted. Her method of adapting was to instruct the student that when they bump into one another off-campus, the student could call her Pam, but when meeting on campus, she preferred to be called "Dr." The provost's experience exemplifies the inner tension many managerial leaders feel. They worked hard to achieve their positions in their respective organizations but feel silly when they insist on being addressed by their titles. She was able to keep institutional decorum and maintain a level of informality.

The fact is that most of today's managers claim it would never have occurred to them to call their coaches, principals, professors, or bosses by their first names. It would have been considered a sign of disrespect.

Another aspect of the experiential bias managers have is related to a tacit understanding of knowing when and how to defer to authority. As one manager put it, "Relational boundaries are very different today. I could never imagine talking to my supervisors the way they talk to me." In the minds of managers, there is a protocol for relating to authority.

Following are a few brief examples from our interviews of how deference to authority does not look like it used to. A manager who has responsibility for hiring in his organization told us that he sometimes wonders if he is conducting the interview or being interviewed by the candidate, "I don't know how it happens but the conversation shifts from me asking, 'Are you right for our company?' to them asking, 'Is your company right for me?'" A professor we interviewed spoke of being admonished on the first day of class by incoming freshmen for selecting a textbook that was both too expensive and hard to read. We even encountered it in a conference where we were speaking in Las Vegas. A Millennial came up after the event and proceeded to critique the presentation and instruct us on how it could be done better. A Baby Boomer waiting behind him was aghast at his comments and interrupted the conversation because she felt the need to apologize for what she perceived to be rudeness on his part. The truth is that the young man made some very astute observations, but the Baby Boomer could not see beyond the inappropriateness of his approach. It is a classic illustration of how the efforts Millennials make to contribute are often misunderstood.

The incidents above are what we refer to as *usurping authority*. It is more than questioning authority—it is about acting as the authority or as an equal. If you work with Millennials, you have experienced it. It feels very abrasive!

SELF-DIFFERENTIATING IS ABOUT YOU

In the opening remarks of this chapter, we use the metaphor of getting hooked as if you are a fish being reeled in by a skillful angler. There is a cast, a tug on the line that creates a reaction, and then the fight is on. Ultimately the fish tires and gives up or breaks the line. Managers who are unaware of their own emotions or how they get triggered can be hooked by the abrasiveness they experience from Millennials.

Whenever we do a consultation with an organization we administer our Generational Rapport Inventory.™ It is a tool we use to measure a manager's strengths and weaknesses with respect to each of the nine competencies. It is interesting that the Communicating competencies (Engaging, Disarming, and Self-Differentiating) are usually the areas in which managers need the most improvement. One explanation we offer is that communication can be challenging in any situation, but when you throw in differing values and attitudes (generational tension), it can become exponentially difficult. Another explanation could be that traditional management training programs were aimed at getting the managers to focus on the followers. In other words, "How can managers get their followers to do what they want them to do?" The relationship between the manager and follower was believed to be negotiated by structure and positional authority.

Sociologist Edwin Friedman and others suggested that managerial leader training programs needed to shift the focus away from the followers, and onto the managers, because it is the nature and presence of a manager that most impacts the followers and the organization. Evidence of the shift of focus in training can be seen in concepts such as Emotional Intelligence, Self-Leadership, and Systems Thinking. Your technical skills allow you to be promoted into management, but your ability to self-regulate and relate to others will determine your level of success. Relationship is not merely a function of structure and power but dependent on a manager's ability to relate to others.

Self-differentiating may be the hardest competency to do well because it demands the most of you. It will also be the most fulfilling because it will impact every area of your life.

KNOW WHERE THEY END AND YOU BEGIN

The key to relational health is self-regulation. All of the toxic forces in life lack self-regulation, from cancerous cells to totalitarian governments—by nature they are invasive of others. Defining the self helps us to not attempt to take others over and not let others take us over. An example of taking others over can be something as simple as not letting people out of a meeting until everyone agrees with you or accusing someone of being disloyal because they see things differently than you. A sign of being taken over by others is when you get reactionary around them and lose your sense of emotional balance. A great term for this is—*someone living in your head rent-free.* We all lose our balance and get hooked emotionally by others. Defining the self requires us to ask, "Why do I need people to agree with me or why am I so bothered by . . . ?"

In the case of the professor whose class did not like the textbook, let us put you in the place of our professor. A great question to ask is, "Why does it bother you that they criticized the textbook you selected?" It is so easy to take the comments others make and personalize them as though they were criticizing you as a person. This is where self-differentiation comes in.

SEPARATENESS AND TOGETHERNESS

There are two great forces in life. There is the force for *Separateness* and the force for *Togetherness*. For personal health, these must be kept in balance. If the force for togetherness is too strong, we tend to lose our objectivity and become enmeshed with the other person or group. This leads to not being able to separate someone else's comment or action from who we are. We personalize the comment or behavior, or as we say, "We take it personally." On the other hand, if the force for separateness is too strong, we have autonomy, but we lose connectivity. We are cut off from the person or group, which is also unhealthy. We become insensitive to their needs and we lose valuable insights they could give us.

KNOW THE DIFFERENCE BETWEEN YOUR ROLE AND YOUR PERSON

Many people confuse their role and their person. You are much greater than your role. It is a part of who you are, but not equal to who you are. When your role is over you still exist. A self-differentiated person understands this and sees the distinction clearly. As a result, even though your role might get criticized or impacted, you can stay intact and in control. If you can maintain your self-differentiated equilibrium when they criticize your direct role, you will have no trouble not taking it personally when the company or organization is criticized or attacked.

BEWARE OF TRIANGULATING

When someone has a problem with someone else, one of the counterproductive ways of handling it is to pull another person into the mix. They are usually neither a part of the problem or the solution, but we pull them in nonetheless for support or to make us feel better about a situation. This is called triangulating. "A" has a problem with "B." A pulls in "C" for moral support or to help in the injustice collecting with regard to B. C now has a problem with B based on A's input. If A's problem with B is solved, C still has a problem with B. Rather than solving the problem, A has allowed the situation to escalate beyond its reasonable proportions. A self-differentiated person has the ability to stay separate when tension arises with another colleague, whether a peer, superior, or a subordinate. They are not enmeshed to the point where they have to involve others in the injustice collecting that leads to villianizing a worker—in this case, a Millennial.

THINK ABOUT YOUR PRESENCE

Think of presence in terms like deep listening, of being open beyond one's preconceptions and biases, and seeing the importance of letting go of old identities and the need to control.[1] Remember it is your presence that most impacts the system. It is not the amount of data you know or your particular skill set. Though important, data and skill sets are merely threshold competencies. They are what get you in the door. They get you your role. As important as they are, it is you as a person who will make all the difference in how you lead and manage. Understanding your presence and its impact is good for managing anybody, but is exponentially important when managing and leading Millennials. A self-differentiated person can distinguish between the anxiety-filled situation and who they are as a person. This allows them to become a "nonanxious" presence in the midst of the storm. Without this awareness, it is easy to take an anxious situation and infuse more anxiety into it, thus making it worse.

Self-differentiation—knowing where you end and others begin—is a key tool in managing others, but more importantly, in managing yourself.

CONFESSIONS

A sports fitness manager said that he used to take it personally when an employee did not pan out. He said that he has learned that people have to be accountable for their own failure or success, "I am accountable for training and pointing them in the right direction, but they have to take it from there." He did say that he is still learning how to not take things personally.

A restaurant manager confesses, "They're still in that egocentric part of their life where it's all about them. I just feel like I'm saying, 'you idiot, of course that's common sense.' So I hate it because I know it's coming out in my tone that way. I really hurt their feelings. I know that they do feel like wow, she's yelling at me again, because I get kind of frustrated sometimes."

Many of the managers in our interviews confessed to having lost their cool, mostly because they were not aware of what hooked them. Another name for "hook" would be pet peeve. Here is a brief list of pet peeves we compiled:

- Not taking responsibility for their actions

- Doing the minimum and not taking ownership

- Projecting blame back onto me

- Having an excuse for everything

- A flippant attitude

- Telling me that I major on the minors

- Not acknowledging the nice things I do for them

- Lack of sensitivity for how difficult my job is

- Quitting without the courtesy of a notice

- A lack of respect

We encourage you to make your own list and then ask yourself why each item is so bothersome to you. A program director for a large leadership training company told us about his office being plagued by high turnover. It was mostly the result of his either canning people or their quitting. We asked him to write down what he thought was a common thread in each of the failed employees. He consented to the exercise and returned with the phrase "poor work ethic" written at the top of his tablet. When we asked whom he used as his benchmark, he replied "Me."

He was not suspending the bias of his experience. More importantly, he was unaware of how his past had forged such a deep-seated frustration with people he deemed to display a lack of *work ethic*. We asked him if he could ever consider himself being a reason for the high turnover. Though surprised, he was intrigued by the question. We probed further by asking him to tell us of when he first realized he had a better work ethic than others around him. "That's easy," he said. He perked up and started telling us that he was the youngest of four boys and could work circles around his older brothers. His countenance shifted and tone lowered, as he began to reflect on how he often had to do their chores as well as his own. He talked about his disappointment in his brothers as adults and attributed their lack of success to work ethic. He blurted, "Wow, at the first sight of any behavior that remotely looks like laziness I react or probably overreact." Now that he is aware of what hooks him, he can modify his behavior by not making snap judgments or writing employees off prematurely.

IN A NUTSHELL

In Chapter 3, we reported what we considered to be differences between managers who were effective at managing Millennials and those who were not. One glaring difference was that the effective managers allowed their subordinates to challenge them. They did not get defensive, they did not get hooked, and they even saw it as a way to connect. They had the ability to self-differentiate and not take personally the complaints, criticisms, and abrasiveness of their younger workers. They realized that the abrasiveness they experienced was not always about them.

Scenario

Dinner for One

Tom was in charge of a high-profile project that could make or break a new line of business for his company. He led a team of 11 employees—all Millennials. His team lived out of a hotel for the life of the three-month project, and he commuted back and forth on weekends to be with his family.

In order to meet project deadlines, the team worked long hours under considerable pressure. When the project was completed successfully and on time, Tom wanted to do something special to reward the team.

He decided to make dinner reservations for his team at one of the finest restaurants in the area. At their debriefing meeting, he congratulated the team and extended an invitation for them to join him for dinner.

(continued)

(*continued*)

One by one they began to text him after the meeting; "Is the dinner mandatory?" "Will it hurt my evaluation if I don't go?" "How long do we have to stay?" "Can I bring a friend?"

Tom was beside himself. He was infuriated. "They are ungrateful. They don't like me. When I was their age, I would have loved to have been invited to dinner with the boss."

Q. If you were Tom, how would you feel? How would you handle this situation? What could help Tom avoid this kind of frustration in the future?

POSTSCRIPT

Tom is a GenX(er). He is highly relational and fun to be around. That is one reason he could not believe his team was not interested in having dinner with him, "I get why they wouldn't want to hang out with my boss but it's me, c'mon." He knew of our work, so he called for advice about what to do with his frustration that was melding into anger. The first thing we said to him was, "Tom relax, it is not about you. You positioned the invitation as a reward, and they just saw it as another work commitment." We talked about the concept of self-differentiating and how he should not take their comments as a personal rejection, but rather as honest sentiments about what they value. Tom heard them saying that they didn't like him, but he could not have been more wrong.

11

THE BIG PICTURE DOES NOT EXIST UNTIL YOU HELP THEM SEE IT

Broadening the Myopic

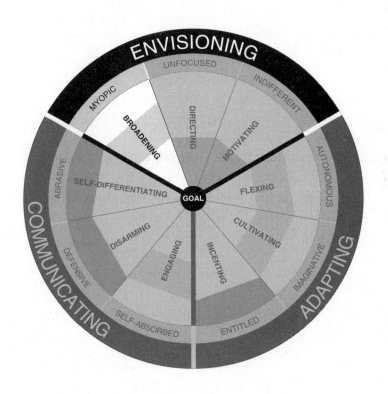

They don't seem to understand the correlation between being kind, efficient, customer focused, and the tip.

—Restaurant Manager

I just try to let them know that our first priority is the customer. If you are late to work or your attitude suffers, it ultimately impacts the shopper's experience. We have jobs because of the customers.

—Grocery Store Manager

He asked me to sponsor him in a 5k that was raising money to fight world hunger. I asked him if he knew what causes world hunger, and he said "no, but I am trying to do my part."

—An Aerospace Manager

You would think the world was coming to an end because I traded shifts with someone who got paid overtime. How was I supposed to know? I am not a payroll expert. I thought I was doing my manager a favor.

—A Millennial

The way to give Millennials the big picture is to engage in a learning process that is involving, presents complexity, and allows the learner to challenge institutional assumptions. By involving, we mean facilitation. The best managers intuitively know this and create orientations, provide training, and teach through *learning activities*. They see their role as key to their employees' success.

Broadening	Myopic
The ability to help Millennials connect the dots between everyday tasks and big picture objectives. Emphasis is placed on teaching employees how to recognize numerous options and potential consequences. It involves teaching organizational awareness.	Millennials struggle with cause-and-effect relationships. The struggle is perceived as a narrow sightedness guided by internal interests without an understanding of how others and the organization are impacted.

Figure 11.1 Broadening the Myopic

THE MILLENNIAL INTRINSIC VALUE

Simplicity. One thing that will ring true to you if you have ever managed Millennials is they will exhaust themselves looking for an easier way to do something. In preparation for a conference, we asked our program director to call the conference coordinator and ascertain where the podium and computer table would be situated in the auditorium in which we would be presenting. After about an hour, we asked if he had the information. He said he did not have it yet. Another hour went by and still no answer. Finally, we asked, "Did you call them?" He replied, "No. I have been searching the conference web site for the room schematics. It is really cool, but I haven't found one for the main auditorium yet." He did not want to play phone tag and thought it would be easier and more efficient to surf for the information. If the world was run by Millennials, his instinct would have been right. But because they do not run the world yet, we asked him to humor us and make the call.

Though Millennials value simplicity, they are not simplistic. Leonardo da Vinci said it best, "Simplicity is the ultimate sophistication."

THE BIAS OF EXPERIENCE

What has become easy for you may not be easy for Millennials. Experience by nature affords us time to see many different facets of our professions, positions, and organizations. What has become clear to experienced managers seems elementary to them, but in reality can be quite complex to others.

The *Harvard Business Review* recently presented a case study involving a Millennial named Josh that perfectly fits the Myopic orientation.[1] The story goes . . . Josh has a marketing idea he has been trying to run by his boss, but his boss keeps putting him off. His boss is frustrated that Josh has energy to come up with new ideas but has not satisfactorily attended to what he is supposed to be doing. Josh is getting increasingly frustrated and is thinking about making an appointment with his supervisor's boss to share his idea. What should Josh do?

If you discuss the case study with Millennials, you will see that they share Josh's frustration about the manager who is holding him back. The one piece of advice that is obvious to you, does not surface in the Millennial conversation: "Don't do it!" It is because you have both organizational and political awareness. You know that it may be job suicide. Millennials do not.

Your bias can cause you to be so frustrated with their lack of awareness and attention to what really matters that you miss the opportunity to paint the big picture for them.

LEARNING FROM SUCCESS

Broadening is an informal means of mentoring or coaching. It does not require a curriculum or regular meeting. It only requires awareness on the part of the manager that an opportunity for facilitating learning has presented itself.

One manager considered teaching consequences to be a part of his job description along with preparing his employees for their futures. "I want them to try to not only do their job for me, but to do it for themselves. I try to instill into their brain that the mistakes they make in the here and now are going to stick with them through their lives. If you constantly call in sick or you don't manage your job in the correct way, it's going to affect you down the road. I tell them, 'If you make this decision, then this is the way it is going to affect you, and here are the repercussions.'" In the vernacular of many managers, they called it "helping Millennials connect the dots."

LEARNING FROM FAILURES

There is a big difference between *helping* Millennials connect the dots and connecting the dots *for* them. The managers who struggled most with broadening understood the need but did not feel that they could commit the time it required of them. Yet, they shared frustration about constantly having to rescue bad decisions and repeatedly explaining the consequences of not thinking about the big picture. The time they spent "teaching" was often confrontational and stress-filled. The experience was unpleasant for both the manager and the Millennial. Some managers we worked with felt uncertain whether they possessed the social skills necessary to "Broaden the Myopic." We suspect many managers used lack of time in their daily schedules to hide their discomfort.

The managers who did prioritize time to participate in their employees' learning considered it to be a valuable investment and an energizing aspect of their job.

START WITH SOMETHING EASY

It is a good idea to practice your broadening skills in a nonthreatening context. One way is simply sharing the information you get. Letting your employees know what is going on the company or at your level of responsibility can help them to think beyond their own cubicle or kiosk. Ask them what they think about the information you share. It is a great way to build trust and a sense of partnership. Everybody likes to be "in" when it comes to information and Millennials are no different.

Orienting employees with the organization's culture is also a good practice. Not with bulky manuals but conversation. Become a storyteller. It helps them interpret symbols, rituals, routines, and informal aspects of working for the company.

Do you know why Starbucks' part-time employees receive 75 percent medical benefits? Howard Schultz says that he had to tenaciously defend the generous benefit while obtaining venture capital for expansion and when taking the company public. The benefit was viewed as being too rich and unheard of for the industry, but Howard considered it to be the soul of Starbucks' commitment to its employees and, therefore, made it off-limits.

But there is a deeper reason for his resolve. He tells of growing up in the projects of Schenectady, New York. Not even a teen yet, he remembered his father announcing at the dinner table that he had lost his job. As that was not sobering enough, Howard's mom told the family she was pregnant. What should have been exciting news was muted by the fact that they had no clear way of seeing how they were going to make it financially, and they had no health care insurance. Howard tells of making the promise that if he were ever in the position to prevent someone from feeling the helplessness he felt, he would make a difference. We can only imagine the myriad of financial adjustments and decisions the company has had to make to stay true to its commitment. Why would someone take the risk of losing venture capital or being downgraded by Wall Street? Things that sometimes seem incredulous make a lot of sense when placed into a context.

THE CONSEQUENTIAL THINKING MODEL

How many times have you asked someone, "Why did you do that?" Only to hear, "I don't know." Managers reported that many of the mistakes Millennials make are the result of not thinking through the consequences that result from their actions. Millennials will catch on quickly to what we call the consequential thinking model. We have talked about how they like to problem solve and use their creative thinking skills. Managers enjoy using the consequential thinking model because they are able to integrate their experience in a nonthreatening way. Let us return to the example of Josh and his marketing idea that we mentioned earlier. Josh is trying to decide if he should do an *end run* and share his idea with his manager's boss.

We would ask Josh to think of three possible options (see Figure 11.2). Let us say that Josh gives us the following three options: (1) I will share my idea with my manager's boss; (2) I will give my manager two more months to set up the meeting; or (3) I will ask

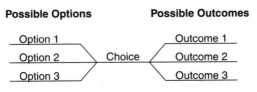

Figure 11.2 The Consequential Thinking Model

my manager why she has not set up the meeting. We would then ask Josh to select one of the three options he has suggested. (Josh has decided to go to his manager's boss because his idea is hot.) Once Josh has made his choice, we would ask him to list three possible outcomes that could result from his action. Josh listed his three outcomes: (1) My manager's boss, loves the idea, promotes me, and I am on my way; (2) my manager's boss asks me why I didn't share my idea with my boss, and I say I did, but she really does not get me—my manager thinks I threw her under the bus, and now I am never going to be promoted; (3) my manager's boss thinks the idea is stupid and asks me not to waste his time ever again. The next stage of the simulation is to ask Josh if he could accept all of the outcomes he listed. If the answer is yes, then Josh is aware of the consequences of his decision and should be prepared to accept whatever happens. If the answer is no, then we would encourage Josh to go back and select a different option and proceed to list three more outcomes.

The consequential thinking model is great for helping people understand both the impact and rippling effect of their actions.

THE FIVE WHYS

Another great exercise for connecting the dots is the "Five Whys."[2] It can be used in a team setting or between a manager and an employee. It is designed to look backward for an understanding of what is happening today. The first *why* is designed to pick the place where you want to begin exploring a particular symptom (we will uses Josh's problem again). The idea is to generate a few possibilities and then use the successive whys (2, 3, 4, and 5) to explore each possibility. Here is how we would help Josh think through his dilemma.

The First Why

Why has Josh's manager not set up a meeting with her boss so that Josh could share his great marketing idea?

- Maybe she is sensitive to her boss's hectic schedule
- Maybe she is trying to protect Josh
- Maybe she does not like the idea

Now select each of the possibilities generated by the first why and then ask whys 2, 3, 4, and 5. To illustrate we select, "Maybe she is trying to protect Josh."

The Second Why

Why is she trying to protect Josh? She is afraid that Josh's idea may get shot down by her boss.

The Third Why

Why is she afraid Josh's idea may get shot down by her boss? Because the timing may not be right for his idea.

The Fourth Why

Why is the timing not right? Because the idea needs more work, and I want to help him with it.

The Fifth Why

Why have you not been able to help him with the idea? Because I have not had the time.

Both exercises are fun, energizing, and designed to shift one- or two-dimensional thinking to the multidimensional realm. The object is to generate several scenarios, options, and possibilities that challenge Millennials to think on a broader scale.

PLEASE, DO SHARE

We are often asked if the economic challenges of the recent past will impact the attitudes Millennials have about work. It is a question that we briefly addressed in Chapter 5. Although the full impact on Millennials is yet to be known, the immediate blow to the Baby Boomers is obvious. They are expected to extend their stay in the workforce due to financial setback. Fifty trillion dollars worth of assets were supporting $25 trillion of debt. The financial bust has depleted those assets so that $25 trillion worth of assets are now supporting $25 trillion of debt. It will not be built back up overnight. Baby Boomers joke that their 401(k)s have become 201(k)s. They will be working because they have to, not because they want to. To them, younger employees will morph from a workplace amusement to an economic threat. Broadening is about giving your knowledge and experience with the goal of developing others. We would be naive to not acknowledge that there are some managers who are afraid to help their underlings connect *all* of the dots for fear of making themselves expendable, as was the case with the following manager that moved us with his story.

He was at the top of his career before the oil bust in the early 1980s. Cutbacks caused him to be displaced by the emergence of a younger, better educated, and cheaper employee. For years, he was bitter. He steadily rebuilt his career but never to the level he had once experienced. He is now nearing 70 years old and still working as a regional sales manager. He spent half a day listening to us talk about how to successfully integrate Millennials into the workplace. At the end of the training, he was generous with his remarks but openly skeptical about the value of younger employees. We asked him to suspend his bias and try the competencies of Engaging and Broadening.

We were surprised to get a phone call from him after a few months. The first words he uttered were, "I get it." He had been witnessing a steady stream of turnover of Millennials in his office. He started to recognize how his boss, himself, and others were making the workplace difficult for his younger co-workers. We asked him if his motivation for maligning the Millennials was residual from his experience of being replaced by someone younger earlier in his career. He did not think so. It was more a difference between what he and his colleagues had to do to get where they are today versus the expectations of the younger workers.

He told us that he has had a change of heart and speaks up for his younger colleagues and considers himself an advocate for them. He is now the go-to-guy when it comes to helping the younger employees. He understands his business better than most, and now his company is truly benefiting from it.

He told us about watching the young guys come and go because they just could not connect the dots. "You can sit at your desk all day making phone calls and e-mailing, but you won't make a sale," he said. He explained that most sales took place early Fridays at the local coffee shops. "Monday through Thursday the customers are in the field putting out fires, but on Friday people grab coffee, secure their orders face-to-face, and then head to the golf course or fishing hole." He encourages his direct reports to keep making calls, but he also invites them to jump in the truck for a Friday morning tour of the coffee shops.

We asked him if his peers questioned his behavior. He told us he was accused of going soft. The fact of the matter, however, is that reaching out to his junior colleagues has resulted in a better work experience for him. He is enjoying work more than ever. He did not say it in as many words, but his self-efficacy has grown.

It is ironic that there was a day when a company thought him to be expendable because of younger employees, and now he is ready to retire, but his company will not let him. He is now inexpendable because of his rapport with younger employees.

He said, "Who says you can't teach an old dog new tricks?" Who says old dogs cannot teach?

IN A NUTSHELL

It has always been true that workers who can share knowledge are disproportionately valuable. But in today's management world, with more than 80 million inexperienced workers entering the ranks, your competitive advantage depends on the ability to share knowledge more than ever before.

Millennials want information shared in simple ways. We are not talking about being simplistic. We are talking about simplicity. We are talking about clarity. Einstein said it well, "Be as simple as possible, but not simpler."

Scenario

Big Picture Thinking on the Big Picture

A good example of an employer of choice is Patagonia. For every one permanent position Patagonia seeks to fill, it receives 900 resumes. The company attributes its low turnover rate (4 percent annually) to the fact that its employees align with the organization's values. A couple of its provocative propositions, "Patagonia exists to effect change on this planet" and "If you don't need our stuff, don't buy it."

One management innovation Patagonia has implemented is what it calls an Enviro Internship. After a full year of employment, an employee can receive full pay for up to 60 days to volunteer for an environmental activist group he or she believes in. The only requirement is that the

(continued)

(*continued*)

employee prepares a report to share what he or she learned with the rest of the company.

Part of Patagonia's turnover is the result of employees returning from an Enviro Internship to announce that they are leaving the company to go to work for the activist group full time. Even when employees defect, Patagonia insists it is part of its mission because the company considers it giving back to the environment.

Q. If you provided internships to your Millennials what would you want them to learn? What do you think of Patagonia's perk? How could your organization benefit as a result of the employee's experience?

12

Ambiguity Is Their Kryptonite

Directing the Unfocused

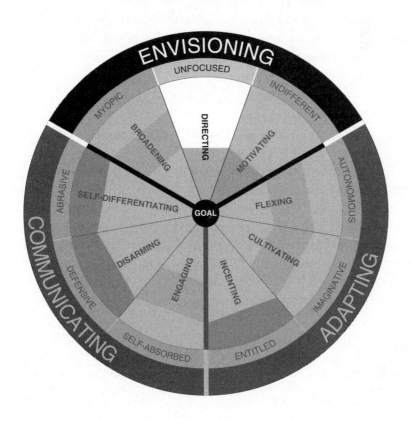

They can be challenging. They definitely need to be guided and kept focused. My job is to keep them focused and keep them on task.

—A Dentist

There are things that I don't feel like I should have to repeat. But I learned that if I want them to get it, I have to tell them over and over.

—A Police Lieutenant

We want clear direction, and then get out of our way.

—A Millennial

Millennials are Super-like. Not unlike the man who wears the big red S on his chest, they too have their kryptonite—it is called ambiguity. They hate ambiguity more than being micromanaged. With insufficient direction, they often exhibit a lack of focus, indecisiveness, and insecurity.

THE MILLENNIAL INTRINSIC VALUE

Millennials are aware that management perceives them as unfocused. They blame the perception on their ability to multitask. They truly believe they can do more than older workers because of their grasp of technology and the speed with which they can access information. Not only do they value doing many different things at once, they value doing many different things. They consider themselves to be focused, but not always on what management wants. They feel uncomfortable with managements' orientation, which

Directing	Unfocused
The ability to clearly communicate what is expected. It entails avoiding ambiguity and not assuming you have been understood. It requires both questioning and listening to ascertain the employee's readiness level for a task or goal.	Millennials, as a cohort, are recognized for their intellectual ability but are often perceived to struggle with a lack of attention to detail. They have a hard time staying focused on tasks for which they have no interest.

Figure 12.1 Directing the Unfocused

they consider to be: "Let's just get things done." Millennials believe that their attention is on personal development and career advancement, but they frequently marshal all of their multitasking skills to focus on what is important to them. That explains why at times you find them giving more attention to things that are not in their job description than the things that are, seemingly unaware that they might be making career-limiting decisions to ignore departmental priorities.

They have been highly attended to as children and therefore do not feel awkward about being given direction, even repeatedly. Although other generations may consider high direction to be micromanagement, Millennials are comfortable as long as it does not come across as condescending or as a response to incompetence.

THE BIAS OF EXPERIENCE

Managers cannot bring themselves to believe that someone can listen to an iPod, manage their fantasy football team, and be focused on work at the same time. Many managers grew up with the mandate that they could not listen to the radio or watch TV while they were studying. It is common today for a junior high student to be talking on their cell phone, Instant Messaging, on their computer, and watching their television while preparing for an exam.

Think about it, over the past two generations we have gone from one phone line per household to one cell phone per family member, plus the old landline. Television has gone from 13 UHF channels to more than 500 via cable or satellite. In 1975, the Internet did not exist, the boom box and Walkman had not yet arrived, no one had a personal computer, and there was no way to record a TV program at home without access to expensive professional equipment. Now we have MP3 players, laptops, notebooks, netbooks, and PCs at home, not to mention a Slingbox and a DVR or two.

At the same time that universities are spending millions to outfit the twenty-first-century classroom with wireless technology, faculty are debating whether they should allow computers in the classroom, "How could they possibly be listening to me if they are gazing at their computer screen?" The sentiment carries over into the boardroom. Many companies restrict the use of smart phones and laptops in meetings.

In both the classroom and boardroom examples, there is an implied understanding that focus has to do with attending to formal authority. It is a residue of the *bureaucratic class*.[1] Managers have learned how to use meetings, budgets, performance evaluation, and organization charts to leverage professional prerogatives and get ahead. Management deems what is important and acts accordingly. While using smart phones, iPods, and tweeting may be symptomatic of attention deficit, the perception that Millennials are unfocused is more related to employees not attending to what is important to management.

The effective managers in our study did not see their focus and the Millennials' focus as mutually exclusive. The key is the ability to link the two.

DIRECTING? I THOUGHT THEY WANTED AUTONOMY

You may be thinking to yourself, "Is it not a contradiction to say that Millennials want both high direction and autonomy?" You will not be the first manager they have left talking to themselves. High achievement is important to them, and they want to know exactly what they have to do to be successful. They fear taking a wrong step or making a bad decision. As a matter of fact, they would rather not make a decision at all than make the wrong decision. Their ability to work in teams often masks their fear of making bad decisions on their own. Working on a team affords Millennials the psychological comfort of sharing the burden of making a mistake.

A manager approached us after a training session to validate the idea that Millennials fear making bad decisions. Her example did not involve an employee but her own son. He had recently graduated with a baccalaureate degree and had interviewed with four different companies. When he called to tell her how the interviews were going, she sensed that he was a little down. She tried to affirm him by saying, "I am proud of you. Just keep lining up the interviews and sooner or later you will get a job." She was shocked when he told her that he had received an offer from each of the companies but wasn't sure which one, if any, he should accept.

When Millennials are unclear about what to do then their multitasking ability can become unfocused and counterproductive. The effective managers were able to help the Millennials see that focusing on organizational objectives and their own objectives were not mutually exclusive. We have noted that Millennials are perceived as autonomous, but that does not mean that they do not welcome direction. After being acknowledged for their ability and potential, they are open to a high level of direction as to how they can go about using their skills.

GIVING DIRECTION

Giving good direction requires flipping the *attending to authority bias* to authority tending to employee development needs. The emphasis is on adapting your management style to the developmental needs of the employee. Through formal or informal conversation, a manager can assess the readiness level of an employee for a particular task, role, or job. The effective managers in our study relied mainly on informal means of assessing their Millennials. Once you know the readiness level of the direct report, you can determine what type of direction needs to be provided. A simple but proven model for ascertaining readiness and directing needs:

1. I explain what I will do

2. I do it and you watch me

3. We do it together

4. You do it and I watch you

5. You do it on your own

6. You explain what you did

The complexity level of a task or goal determines how much time is required for directing. Good direction includes telling and showing people what to do, when to do it, how to do it, and providing timely feedback on results.

The effective managers in our study shifted the focus from *perform for me* to *let's partner for performance*. It is important for manager and employee to find agreement about what is helpful to develop both parties' competencies. Partnering for performance requires that consideration and balance be given to the manager's goals, the Millennial's goals, and the organization's goals.

LEARNING FROM SUCCESS

You will find some good strategies for partnering for performance in the following advice we received from the managers in our study.

Make It about Their Success

In Chapter 3, we talked about the primary differences we observed between the effective and challenged managers in our study. The Holy Grail to managing Millennials is seeing yourself as key to their success. The effective managers considered themselves successful when their Millennial employees experienced success.

Focus on the Mission

There has been an emphasis over the past 20 years or so on the importance of creating organizational mission, vision, and value statements. Several managers in our study spoke of such statements as boundaries for both their own behavior and the behavior of their employees. One of our interviewees eloquently voiced the perspective of managers who recognized the importance of staying within those boundaries, while simultaneously directing younger employees, when he told us: "But so long as individuals are moving in favor of mission, vision, and values, then I am open to adapting to the uniqueness of the people that work with me." By focusing on mission, vision, and values, the conversation about developmental needs moves beyond what we each want to what the organization needs from all of us.

Let Them Try Other Things

A common theme in our interviews was how quickly Millennials get bored with their job description. It is a conundrum of sorts because you want to oblige their need for personal development, but you still need someone to perform certain routine tasks. Managers commented, "There's a job at hand, and while you might like to do those other things, you can't do those things until you actually do your job. And if there's time, then we'll let you do those things." Great managers anticipate when their employees need a new challenge and try to create opportunities for them before they become *unfocused*. Competencies like Engaging and Cultivating are useful for staying one-step ahead of their boredom.

Millennials respond well to cross-training programs. They are stimulated by the change of environment and routine.

Let Them Make Mistakes

Opportunities to give direction often present themselves when mistakes are made. Giving someone the space to fail at a task or goal can be just as important to his or her development as formal training. "I try to give guidance and advice knowing the outcome and the goal that has to happen. But I try to leave room for my staff to make mistakes. None of us is perfect. One way to get better is to learn from our mistakes. But obviously mistakes can only happen to a certain level, so I am also here as a safety net to get things back on track if necessary."

LEARNING FROM OUR FAILURES

When speaking of their own failures, a common theme in our manager interviews was the mistake they referred to as, "assuming too much."

Do Not Assume They Know What to Do

Many managers felt that their organizations did not make a big enough commitment to training. "I wish we had a little more supervision in each department. We could do a better job of training. I think if they feel like they know what is expected and equipped to do it, they would do a better job and stay longer." They talked about the need to focus on small, almost trivial, details. A Golf Pro offered an example, "We should have monthly trainings on something as small as the proper way to drive a golf cart from the clubhouse to the parking lot." The point is that you cannot assume that they know what to do. Several managers said they are reluctant to give high direction because they consider some things a matter of common sense. The term "common sense" consists of what people in common would agree on. But Millennials are not *in common* with the other age cohorts, and they often need a much greater level of clarity and direction than managers typically expect.

Do Not Assume They Heard You the First Time

We made a big deal out of the Millennial's ability to multitask at the beginning of this chapter. Most studies on multitasking do not address the Millennial age cohort in particular, but evidence suggests that comprehension, reaction time, quality of work, and memory are all severely impacted by it. Russell Poldrack, professor of psychology at UCLA, published findings on how multitasking affects the brain's learning systems, and as a result, he found that we do not learn as well when we are distracted. Poldrack warns that managers need to be aware that "... multitasking adversely affects how you learn. Even if you learn while multitasking, that learning is less flexible and more specialized, so you cannot retrieve the information as easily."

So there. You are not crazy. The good news, however, is that not all tasks require the same level of attention. In 2007, the *Harvard Business Review* recognized Linda Stone for coining the phrase "continuous partial attention" to describe fragmented focus demanded by the hectic workplaces many of us occupy. There is considerable debate as to the effects of this condition, but most of us would agree that there is a benefit to being able to take a quick call, text message, or e-mail to keep an important project on track. The challenge for managers is to ascertain when multitasking is interfering with training, learning, and other tasks that require a higher level of focus.

IN A NUTSHELL

Millennials welcome high direction. Clear and repetitive instruction is important. If you sense that your direct report is anxious or distant, it may be because of a lack of clarity or understanding of what is required from her or him.

Scenario

Manager as Career Coach

One manager (Kim) we interviewed talked about the need to "go slow to go fast." You cannot turn them loose too fast.

(continued)

(*continued*)

She talked about learning her trade when she was first entering the workforce. "It was kind of like fly or die." Kim obviously learned how to fly, but today she thinks coaching and feedback could have made a huge difference early in her career. She considers it her duty to do for her direct reports what no one did for her. She referred to herself as a kind of career coach.

In Kim's opinion, today's younger employees are afraid to fail and sometimes that inhibits their decision making. "They seem to be uncomfortable with ambiguity and want a sure thing." Here are six of her tips: (1) "uh huh" is not a yes, (2) never assume your directions are understood—ask clarifying questions, (3) give formal and informal feedback as quickly as possible—immediate feedback is important, (4) once you are certain your direction is understood—get out of the way, (5) get agreement about outcome expectations, (6) always be prepared with the next thing for your younger employees—they thrive on challenge.

Q. What would turning someone loose too fast look like to you? How frequently do you deliver formal and informal feedback? What do you think of Kim's concept of manager as career coach?

13

THEY WANT TO KNOW "WHY" BEFORE "WHAT"

Motivating the Indifferent

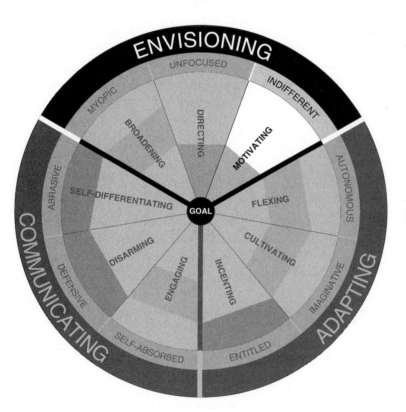

They just don't seem to care about customers.

—A Fast Food Manager

A lot of kids my age really want their work to mean something. If they feel like they are making a measurable difference, and if they're told that they're making that difference, that's when they really seem to buy in. I like that because I'm the same way. I want to make a difference, too.

—A Community Center Manager

They offered me a big promotion, but I am not sure I want them to get their claws that deep into me. Most of the managers here look pretty unhappy to me.

—A Millennial

It is not your responsibility as a manager to give someone meaning; you need only to help them find it.

THE MILLENNIAL INTRINSIC VALUE

Millennials want, no, *need* to find meaning in their work. Early in our research process, we were using the term "apathetic" rather than "indifferent." That is until we interviewed a young social entrepreneur. When he showed up, he told us we could only have 15 minutes, less than half the time for which we had prepared. During the first few minutes of the interview, he was polite but not very engaged, and then he saw a term we used in our research— apathy. He said, "Apathy? My generation is not apathetic. We care

Motivating	Indifferent
The ability to inspire Millennials to find meaning in the everyday work they do and to see how their contribution matters.	Millennials are perceived as careless, apathetic, or lacking commitment.

Figure 13.1 Motivating the Indifferent

deeply about a lot of things. We just need a reason to care! Apathy is the wrong word." He suggested we use the word "indifferent" (meaning neutral). He ended up giving us almost two hours of his time and then he said, "You should have told me what you were trying to do. This is kind of cool." In Millennial speak that means— you should have given me a reason to care.

Further investigation reveals that Millennials do care deeply about many things. The Higher Education Research Institute (HERI) at UCLA reported that the entering freshmen class of 2005 showed a distinctive and widespread rise in attitudes reflecting social concerns and civic responsibility behaviors compared with previous cohorts. Two out of three (66.3 percent) report they believe it is essential or very important to help others who are in difficulty, the highest this figure has been in the past 25 years. An all-time high of 83.2 percent report that they volunteered at least occasionally during their high-school senior year and 70.6 percent report that they typically volunteered on a weekly basis. Also at an all-time high is the percentage of students who believe there is a very good or some chance that they will participate in volunteer or community service in college, at 67.3 percent.[1] It has been reported that the largest club at Harvard Business School is The Social Enterprise Club. Also, 15 percent of a recent Princeton graduation class applied to Teach For America, a program in which you spend your first two years of teaching in inner city or rural schools. Interestingly, *BusinessWeek* ranked Teach For America #7 in the top #100 places to start a career.[2]

Some experts explain the rise in social awareness as a result of high schools emphasizing voluntarism in the curriculum and universities using it as criteria for acceptance. The HERI report suggested that the jump in social concern was in part a reaction to the worst global and national disasters witnessed in their lifetime. Two examples that occurred during their high school years are the Indian Ocean tsunami and Hurricane Katrina.

It is not just college kids. The receptionist at a country club presented her boss with the idea of collecting food from the membership through the holiday season to help people who were in need. He told her that she would have to organize and execute the food drive on her own because of a lack of staff and the busyness of the season. She consented to take on the project and collected thousands of dollars in food. She was honored with the *employee of the year* award but blushes when you ask her about it. She beams when you ask her what she most likes about her job and says, "I can make a difference."

THE BIAS OF EXPERIENCE

"Nobody gave us a reason to care and we liked it!" Okay, that might be a bit over the top but, as one older manager put it, "Getting a paycheck was meaning enough." One focus group of managers could not stop laughing at the comment made by a Builder manager, "My motivation for being to work by 8 o'clock every morning was that work started at 8 o'clock in the morning." You can imagine the floodgate of sentiments that followed. Being grateful to have a job, work ethic, and pleasing the boss were at the heart of the conversation. We saw this scene repeated again and again with all of our focus groups.

In Chapter 2, we talked about the notion that the time in which you were born and the events that take place in society during your adolescence help to shape your values, attitudes, and beliefs. We would like to take you back to Psychology 101 and revisit Maslow's Hierarchy of Needs (see Figure 13.2).

Maslow claimed that individuals' higher order needs only come into focus when lower order needs are satisfied. Physiological needs consist of food, water, clothing, shelter, and sleep. Safety needs include employment, physical safety, the family, and property. Belonging needs are comprised of friendship, love, and family. Esteem needs include self-esteem, confidence, achievement, and respect of others. Self-actualization needs encompass self-fulfillment, creativity, spontaneity, and problem solving.

The Hierarchy of Needs model was developed to explain individual motivation, but we find the concept useful in explaining

Figure 13.2 Maslow's Hierarchy of Needs

differences among the generations in their orientations toward the workplace. The four generations in the workplace today entered their work lives at different places on the hierarchy due to societal change. The Builders arrived to work at the *safety* level. They are likely to say, "Why isn't a paycheck enough to motivate someone?" The Baby Boomers entered between the *belongingness* and *esteem* levels. They love club life and titles. They are likely to say, "Listen, be patient, do your time, and you too can be partner." GenX(ers) started at the *esteem* level. Belonging is a given to them and they prefer a meritocracy. They are likely to say, "I value work-life balance, too, but show me what you can do and we will talk." Are you ready? Millennials are entering between the *esteem* and *self-actualization* levels. They are likely to say, "I want to bring my creativity to work, problem solve, and find meaning in what I do."

As people solve lower order problems, they may become discontented about higher order issues. It is paradoxical but improvement in human affairs often leads not to satisfaction but to discontent. It is discontent that motivates us to change. Maslow would say, "Don't evaluate your organization on whether there is discontent or no discontent. Evaluate it on the quality of discontent." It is a poor quality of discontent when employees feel they are not safe at work. We would say that the quality of discontent is high when employees complain of "not seeing their imprint" on a product or service. When employees strive to find meaning in their work, it is the difference between the *Grapes of Wrath* and Google. John Steinbeck's novel is set in a time when companies exploited their workers and the discontented response took the form of unions. At Google headquarters in Mountain View, the company provides on-site oil change, car wash, dry cleaning, massage therapy, gym, hair stylist, fitness classes, and bicycle repair.[3]

HIERARCHY OF CAPABILITIES

Gary Hamel, management innovation guru, challenges, "We have to reinvent our management systems, so they inspire human beings to bring all their capabilities to work every day."[4] He created a hierarchy of human capability that contributes to competitive success:

Obedience: Taking direction and following rules

Diligence: Being accountable and not taking shortcuts

Intellect: Smart, eager to improve skills, and willing to borrow ideas from others

Initiative: Do not wait to be told and seek out new ways to add value

Creativity: Inquisitive, irrepressible, and not afraid to say stupid things

Passion: Climb over obstacles and refuse to give up

Hamel measures the contribution of each of the capabilities to what he calls value creation.

Passion	35%
Creativity	25%
Initiative	20%
Intellect	15%
Diligence	5%
Obedience	0%
	100%

Although he gave obedience a score of zero, he contends that obedience is worth something, because if people did not follow rules, chaos would emerge. He explains, "When it comes to value creation or competitive success, rule-following employees don't contribute. Value creation is primarily the product of passion and creativity."

Millennials find meaning in value creation particularly through the capabilities of creativity and passion. But managers may put more emphasis on the obedience, diligence, and experience capabilities. In the old school, employees were expected to work their way up the value creation hierarchy in the same way that individuals must meet physiological needs before they can address safety needs in Maslow's hierarchy. Many managers today would still like to see Millennials master the lower levels of Hamel's Hierarchy of Human Capability (i.e., obedience and diligence) before they are allowed to offer their creativity and passion. The danger is that a manager so focused on the rule-based approach might just miss the great potential that Millennials have in the area of passion, creativity, initiative, and intellect.

The Massive Middle

Recently, organizations have been paying a lot of attention to the idea of *employee engagement*. Engagement gauges the level of connection employees feel with their employer, as demonstrated by their willingness and ability to help their company succeed. In 2007, Towers Perrin, a consulting firm, conducted a worldwide study of almost 90,000 participants on workforce attitudes.[5]

They measured what they call the head, hands, and heart. The "head" refers to how employees rationally connect with their company's goals and values. The "hands" refers to the employee's willingness to put in a great deal of extra effort to help the company succeed. And the "heart" is the emotional connection between employee and employer. The sum total of the three elements is what was used to measure overall employee engagement levels.

The study shows that barely one in five employees (21 percent) is fully engaged on the job. And 8 percent are fully disengaged. This means that an overwhelming 71 percent of employees fall into what they call the "massive middle" who are neither engaged or disengaged. They are indifferent.

Here are some signs of indifference:

- Often feel unable to commit to tasks that hold little meaning for them.

- They have strong reservations about jobs they are asked to do; as a result, they approach them half-heartedly.

- Rather than acknowledging a problem and taking steps to correct it, they convince themselves that the problem does not exist.

- They are often plagued with feelings of anxiety, uncertainty, anger, frustration, and alienation.

Keep Them Engaged and Out of the Middle

In Chapter 6, we emphasized the competency of matching extrinsic rewards (bonuses, raises, praise, promotions, etc.) to Millennial values. The focus here is on the importance of recognizing the satisfaction Millennials get from performing well and feeling like they made a contribution to the organization (intrinsic rewards).

When we use the phrase "motivate the indifferent," we are not suggesting that you can put motivation into unmotivated people. It is a fruitless exercise and usually ends with the manager frustrated. However, you can create an environment conducive to self-motivation.

LEARNING FROM SUCCESS

Managers who were able to create atmospheres in which Millennials take initiative provide meaningful challenges, freedom of personal choice in how they pursue the challenges, and a sense of urgency about the meaning of their work to the organization.

Why Is It Worth Doing?

Millennials want to know *why* before *what*. They ask *why* as a means of placing value on the activity. A marketing manager had asked her direct report to make 300 copies of a market study and was taken aback when asked *why*. The *why* was not in defiance but a fishing expedition of sorts. The objective in the mind of the direct report was to ascertain what role she was playing in the grand scheme of things.

We met some incredible motivators and one thing they all had in common was they were convinced of their own purpose and could articulate the *why* and the value their employees brought to the *why*. A community center director gave the example of when one of his Millennials wanted to quit, "I told him you're here because you care. These kids look up to you. If it weren't for these kids having the challenges that they have, we wouldn't be needed. There would be no reason for our organization. If they had perfect home lives and they were perfect at school, then why be here?" His employee responded, "We can do this, we can make a difference in these kids' lives. I won't be doing this forever but while I am here I am all in!"

Meaningful challenge can be as simple as explaining *the meaning of their work* before *explaining the how.* Like the old proverb, "Before you ask men to gather lumber to build a ship let them acquire a love for the sea."

Allowing for Personal Choice

Some may read *personal choice* and think autonomy, but it is so much more than autonomy. It is allowing Millennials to think about what they best contribute to value creation. Here are some great questions to help Millennials process personal choice:[6]

What do you most need from your work?

What makes for a really good day?

What would you miss if you left this job?

What did you like best about other jobs you have had?

How do you most like to spend your time outside of work?

Tell me about a time you felt most energized at work?

Creating a Sense of Urgency

Actually, it is more like managing a sense of energy. Millennials already have a sense of urgency about their own development and personal goals. The effective managers were able to help Millennials see the organization's goals as an extension of their personal goals. Managing a sense of urgency requires reconciling employee effort to desired organizational outcomes through frequent communication.

LEARNING FROM OUR FAILURES

It is not uncommon to hear managers say, "People are our greatest asset." The importance of valuing your employees is well documented. But if you are not careful, it is easy to give affirmation to technology and process at the expense of people.

Praise People, Not Technology

One way to deflate someone, who is bringing creativity and passion to a project, is to compliment the technology he or she uses and not the person. As technology has advanced, it has become easier and easier to misappropriate credit. Because of their technological savvy, this misappropriation commonly happens to Millennials. Perhaps you have done it yourself, "The copies are already on my desk? That new copier is the best investment we ever made!" "The report looks incredible! That desktop publishing program could make anyone look like a graphic designer." "You collected on 80 percent of our receivables? Wow, what would we do without our billing software?" The problem with praising technology is that it will not work any harder nor think of ways it can make a greater contribution.

Do Not Put the "What" before the "Why"

One of the biggest mistakes a manager can make is to be dismissive of the *why*. Believe it or not, we have encountered managers who do not think it is important to explain the *why*. In their opinion, if they ask for 300 copies, that should be enough motivation.

IN A NUTSHELL

You have to help Millennials find a reason to care. They are the easiest of the workforce to motivate once you have helped them find meaning in what they do. You keep them motivated by letting them see how what they do matters. They thrive in an atmosphere of change—not because of change itself, but because they get to put their mark on the future.

The following scenario illustrates how a Millennial who already finds meaning in her work can be demotivated by a manager who does not allow her to bring her creativity and passion to the job.

Scenario

The Storm after Katrina

Jennifer, having recently graduated from college with an accounting degree, was watching television and just could not get the pictures of Hurricane Katrina's devastation out of her mind. She was so moved by the images that she decided to give the first year of her work life to helping with the recovery effort.

Jennifer applied to a nonprofit relief agency and was hired. Her compensation entailed a place to live and a modest stipend for food. She was excited about doing something with her life that would be meaningful.

When she arrived in New Orleans, she discovered that most of her team was made up of people her age who shared the same ideal of making a difference. Jennifer said, "Within a month, we were all demoralized. Not because of the challenges a recovery effort presents but because of our supervisor." She went on to explain that her manager invited their opinions but never acted on them. "He said we were a team but he pretty much made all of the decisions on his own," she said. Jennifer and the others had skills and competencies that the manager never utilized.

Jennifer summarized, "I think it would have been a much more meaningful experience had we gotten to participate in decision making and strategizing. I am still glad I went!"

Q. What could Jennifer's manager have done differently? Do you find that your direct reports like to participate in brainstorming or decision making? In what ways do managers give their direct reports a reason not to care?

PART

III

YOUR COMPETITIVE ADVANTAGE

CHAPTER

14

BUILDING A MILLENNIAL-FRIENDLY CULTURE

Here we must resist the temptation to say, "It all starts at the top. If the executives do not embrace 'Building a Millennial-Friendly Culture' in some sort of large-scale change initiative it won't work." Sure, executives ought to be thinking about the future of their organizations and the role Millennials will be playing in them. They should also be preparing to train and equip managers with the skills necessary to engage Millennials. But we remain true to our introductory remarks. The lead character in our story is the manager.

IDENTIFY YOUR ALL-STARS AND GIVE THEM A PLATFORM

A huge emphasis has been placed on knowledge sharing over the past couple of decades. As a result of the emphasis, organizations have become more innovative, more productive, and more profitable. If you were to analyze peer knowledge that actually gets shared in organizations, you would discover that it rarely includes managerial best practices. If you recall from the description of our study, human resources (HR) knew whom to select for both the effective and challenged manager groups, but struggled to explain what managerial competencies differentiated its selections. We think it is because our systems are built to deal with problem people and not all-stars. As long as there are no complaints about a manager, all is well. Perhaps you cannot offer the amount of time it takes to deal with problem managers but identifying all-stars and giving them a platform is the quickest and most effective way to make your culture Millennial-friendly. We offer our findings as evidence that you probably have experts in your own organization.

Another barrier to identifying all-stars is that most people who are good at something think it is easy and therefore they believe anyone can do it. Even if people recognize their own success, they are reluctant to take the role of an authority for fear of hazing or criticism by colleagues. But think about it. If one manager had information that could favorably impact the outcome of a client's decision and did not share it with the colleague making the presentation, it would be viewed as harmful to the company. The manager in question would never be able to excuse her action by saying, "Sharing information is a very personal thing, and I don't feel that I am in a place to give useful information to another manager. Besides, what if someone thinks I am full of myself?" Create an environment in which managers are comfortable to share what works for them. It could be something as easy as giving space on the weekly meeting agenda to ask, "What worked for you this week?"

Almost all organizations have incorporated the practice of reviewing "lessons learned" at the end of a project cycle, and many organizations have embraced the concept so thoroughly that it shows up in all kinds of nonproject areas. "Lessons learned" has become a safe banner under which to critique decisions that probably should have been made differently, as well as to emphasize what was done right. We suggest that effective managerial practices be added to the list of innovations to watch out for.

If you are one of those managers who are good at managing Millennials, do not wait for someone to give you a platform. You owe it to your colleagues to share your knowledge. If you are frustrated with managing Millennials, find another manager inside or outside of your organization you believe to be effective. Observe what they do. Pick their brain and do not let them "awe shucks" you.

INVOLVE YOUR MANAGERS IN THE CONVERSATION

If you are going to implement a program at a company-wide level, whether it is a formal task force or an informal series of brown-bag sessions, make sure that the people who manage Millennials are at the table and given a voice. In many cases, upper-management may be several levels removed from what is really happening with respect to integrating Millennials. When you invite the managers to the conversation, ask them to bring a Millennial.

ASK MILLENNIALS

When all else fails, ask the Millennials. Observe them at the doctor's office, grocery store, or restaurant, and ask them what they like best about their manager. Sit down with the Millennials in your organization and ask them to help you design the kind of organization in which they want to work. The activity in and of itself is Millennial-friendly. Revisit the list of intrinsic values and brainstorm about how they can best be reflected in your organization. Think in terms of recruiting, compensating, handbooks, policies, procedures, polity, and organizational structure.

Millennial Intrinsic Values

Work-Life Balance

Reward

Self-Expression

Attention

Achievement

Informality

Simplicity

Multitasking

Meaning

SUSPEND ORGANIZATIONAL BIAS

Not unlike individuals, organizations also have biases. We received a call from a law firm in the Southern California region. The firm manager heard us speak at a conference and had engaged us to work with the partners in the firm. They were experiencing a regular exodus of young attorneys. The exit interviews produced similar sentiments, "I am leaving for another firm that has a development plan for my career." The fact is the young attorneys wanted assurances that if they put in the work, they would get the reward. Before the first meeting, the firm manager called and apologized but asked if we would be willing to be on a conference call with the senior partner because he had some questions. The call did not last long. The senior partner started by saying, "You are not telling me that we have to change what has worked for us for over 50 years are you?" Let it suffice to say that "maybe" did not cut it. We tried asking him to "suspend the bias," but he was not having any of it.

A school system we worked with recognized that there was bias in its system as to how one could become the principal of a school. It were getting fewer and fewer candidates because its process required that a person first serve as an assistant principal. It makes sense that you would want someone to be an assistant first, but there are assumptions of readiness that may or may not be true. Many people who would make great principals were not interested in being assistant principals. The school district supervisors were able to suspend their bias and are now looking at alternative ways for people to become principals.

You cannot talk about culture without talking about symbols. The corporate ladder itself is a symbol of bias. It consists of a traditional hierarchy with a singular path upward along which employees either move up or stop moving, presumes a certain work-versus-life balance orientation, and assumes workers' needs remain consistent over time. It has adversely impacted women for decades. As workers needs are changing, new paradigms are emerging. Cathleen Benko and Anne Weisberg talk about the need for organizations to move to a corporate lattice. A lattice has multiple paths upward, allows a choice between moving faster or slower, or even a change of directions, provides for career-life fit, and adjusts as workers' needs change over time.[1]

There are all kinds of bias in organizational culture and that is not always bad. Just look for areas where it may be inhibiting participation by or the upward mobility of Millennials.

PROMOTE THE CORE COMPETENCIES FOR MANAGING TODAY'S WORKFORCE

Our answer to the question, "What differentiates managers who are effective from those who struggled" is the nine competencies. The key to building a Millennial-friendly culture is to promote the core competencies. The good news is that the competencies are not based on personality and they can be learned.

We hope you have found our descriptions of the competencies required to manage the Millennials to be helpful. And we hope that you will be excited to know that the real power of our model is yet to be unveiled—the competencies are measurable! While conducting our research, we noticed that all of the managers in our study were doing at least one thing right. However, many were not sure about what they were doing right or wrong. The uncertainty caused them to be inconsistent in the way they managed. We thought that if managers could know what they were doing right and wrong, they could more easily and readily adapt their management style. Knowing what to do and not do with respect to successful performance leads to self-efficacy. A key indicator of a person's future success is self-efficacy. Managerial leaders who achieve self-efficacy lead to Millennials who achieve self-efficacy! See Figure 14.1.

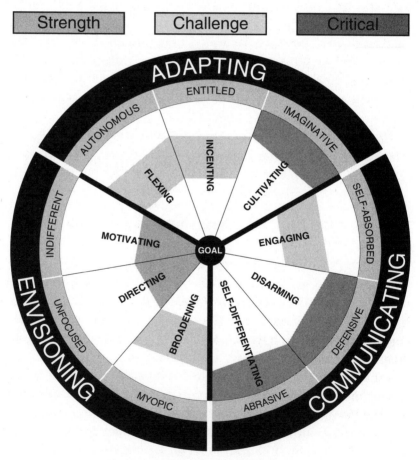

Figure 14.1 Generational Rapport Inventory Graph

THE GENERATIONAL RAPPORT INVENTORY

We created the Generational Rapport Inventory™ (GRI) to help managers ascertain their developmental level with respect to the nine core competencies. The GRI measures your thinking, your self-reported behavior, and the perception of your direct reports. We measure thinking and behaving separately to determine if you need to adapt to a new perspective, learn new behaviors, or both. For most of us, the kind of thinking and skills that got us to where we are today may be the things that are holding us back from continued personal growth and effectiveness. In figure 14.1, the dark gray area represents a critical need for development, light gray indicates a challenge area, and medium gray signifies an area of strength.

In addition to identifying areas of strength and challenge, the GRI can reveal where the greatest point of tension lies between you and your direct reports. Tension is the first stage of conflict. The best way to reduce tension is to communicate. Unfortunately, many people do not communicate because they cannot put their finger on what is wrong. By identifying potential tension, you can have a conversation that alleviates conflict and builds rapport.

The GRI Composite Report

Every organization should have a training budget. More importantly, every organization should know where training would most impact its effectiveness and productivity. The GRI Composite is a divining rod of sorts that identifies areas of need for training. Once your managers have taken the GRI, we can show where the organization is strong or weak with respect to the core competencies that are critical to managing Millennials.

Our model does not require that you reinvent the wheel. Nor is it the flavor of the month. We can help you integrate previous training and repurpose it with the nine competencies. If you have already invested in Situational Leadership training or Emotional Competency training, both teach skills that are critical to managing Millennials.

The GRI Offer

Since you have made it to the end of the book, we want to reward you by extending an invitation for you to take a modified version of the Generational Rapport Inventory. It only takes about 10 minutes and it is online. On completion you will immediately be e-mailed a link to your report. The report will score your *thinking* with relationship to the nine competencies.

You may access the GRI online at www.genextconsulting.com.

Training and Consulting

If you are interested in making *Managing the Millennials* a training priority for your company, please contact:

Red Tree Leadership
(800) 851-9311
www.redtreeleadership.com

In the End

We hope our book helps managers feel more competent, better equipped, and more relaxed so that they can enjoy their Millennials. We believe the nine competencies will help create environments in which both managers and Millennials will thrive. Just as we wish success to each individual and organization we work with, we wish it for you and your organization. For the Millennial generation we have a special wish—make our organizations better. They are the future. They are our future.

Chapter 1 The Millennials and You

1. Nadira Hira, "Attracting the twentysomething worker," *Fortune Online*, May 15, 2007, http://money.cnn.com/magazines/fortune/fortune_archive/2007/05/28/100033934/index.htm.
2. C. Hirschman, "Here they come," *Human Resource Executive,* (July 2006): 22.
3. J. Estrin, *Closing the Innovation Gap: Reigniting the Spark of Creativity in a Global Economy* (New York: McGraw-Hill, 2009, p. 56).
4. Hudson Institute (2003).
5. K. Dychtwald, T. J. Erickson, and R. Morison, *Workforce Crisis: How to Beat the Coming Shortage of Skills and Talent* (Boston, Mass achusetts: Harvard Business School Press, 2006).
6. G. Cole, R. Smith, and L. Lucas, "The Debut of Generation Y in the Workplace," *Journal of Business Administration Online,* Retrieved October 21, 2005, from http://www.atu.edu/business/jbao/Menu/fall2002.htm
7. J. M. Twenge, *Generation Me: Why Today's Young Americans Are More Confident, Assertive, Entitled—and More Miserable than Ever Before* (New York: Free Press, 2006).
8. Lee Hecht Harrison Survey (2006).

Chapter 2 Aren't We All Just the Same?

1. Incidentally, that is the question when speaking of any type of diversity—really, aren't we all the same?

2. E. Thelen and K. E. Adolph, Arnold L. Gesell, *Developmental Psychology, 28* (3) (1992): 368-380.

3. H. Schultz and D. J. Yang, *Pour Your Heart into It: How Starbucks Built a Company One Cup at a Time* (1st ed.) (New York: Hyperion, 1997).

4. J. Pilcher, "Mannheim's Sociology of Generations: An Undervalued Legacy," *British Journal of Sociology 45* (3) (1994): 481-494.

5. C. Bollas, *Being a Character: Psychoanalysis and Self Experience* (1st ed.) (New York: Hill and Wang, 1992).

6. S. Biggs, "Thinking about Generations: Conceptual Positions and Policy Implications," *Journal of Social Issues 63* (4) (2007): 695-711.

7. R. A. Settersten and K. U. Mayer, "The Measurement of Age, Age Structuring, and the Life Course," *Annual Review of Sociology (1997): 23*: 233.

8. N. B. Ryder, "The cohort as a concept in the study of social change," *American Sociological Review, 30* (6) (1965): 843-861.

9. M. W. Riley, "On the Significance of Age in Sociology," *American Sociological Review, 52* (1) (1987): 1-14.

Chapter 4 The Points of Tension between Managers and Millennials

1. V. Büsch, S. Dahl, and D. Dittrich, "Age Discrimination in Hiring Decisions: A Comparison of Germany and Norway," *Institute for Research in Economics and Business Administration,* December, 2004.

2. T. D. Nelson, (Ed.) *Ageism: Stereotyping and Prejudice against Older Persons* (Boston: MIT Press, 2002).

3. F. Popcorn, *The Popcorn Report: Faith Popcorn on the Future of Your Company, Your World, Your Life* (New York: Doubleday, 1991, p. 57).

4. L. T. O'Brien and M. L. Hummert, "Memory Performance of Late Middle-Aged Adults: Contrasting Self-Stereotyping and Stereotype Threat Accounts of Assimilation to Age Stereotypes," *Social Cognition 24* (3) (2006): 338.

5. T. Schmader, "Gender Identification Moderates Stereotype Threat Effects on Women's Math Performance," *Journal of Experimental Social Psychology 38* (2002): 194–201.

6. A. A. Nease, B. O. Mudgett, and M. A. Quiñones, "Relationships among Feedback Sign, Self-efficacy, and Acceptance of Performance Feedback," *Journal of Applied Psychology 84* (5) (1999): 806-814.

7. A. Bandura, *Social Foundations of Thought and Action: A Social Cognitive Theory* (Englewood Cliffs, N.J.: Prentice Hall, 1986).

Chapter 6 Rewarding the Right Things in the Right Ways

1. S. McManus and S. Sabol, (Producers) *Inside the NFL* television series. New York: HBO Sports, November 2007.
2. J. M., Beyer and others, "The Selective Perception of Managers Revisited," *Academy of Management Journal, 40* (3): 716-737.
3. B. Nelson and P. Economy, Business Pro—York University, Books24x7—York University, and Books24x7, I. *The Management Bible* (Hoboken, N.J.: John Wiley & Sons, Inc., 2005).
4. N. Shawchuck, "Leadership and Community," (lecture at Southern California College, Costa Mesa, CA, September 1993).

Chapter 7 They Are at the Head of the Creative Class

1. A. Campbell, J. Whitehead, and Finkelstein, "When Good Leaders Make Bad Decisions," *Harvard Business Review*.
2. Peter Gruber, quoted in A. Muoio, ed., "My greatest lesson." *FastCompany*.
3. J. Lipman-Blumen and H. J. Leavitt, *Hot Groups: Seeding Them, Feeding Them, and Using Them to Ignite Your Organization* (New York: Oxford University Press, 1999).

Chapter 8 First Them, Then You

1. www.drspock.com/about/drbenjaminspock/0,1781,00.html.
2. M. J. Wheatley, *Turning to One Another: Simple Conversations to Restore Hope to the Future* (2nd ed.) (San Francisco, California; London: Berrett-Koehler, McGraw-Hill distributor, 2009, p. 30).
3. T. Rath, *Vital Friends: The People You Can't Afford to Live Without* (New York: Gallup Press, 2006, p. 62).
4. L. Branham, *The 7 Hidden Reasons Employees Leave: How to Recognize the Subtle Signs and Act Before It's Too Late* (New York: American Management Association, 2005).

Chapter 9 Fragile, Handle with Care

1. D. Sacks, "Scenes from the culture clash: Companies are just now waking up to the havoc that the newest generation of workers is causing in their offices." *FastCompany*, 2006.
2. G. A. Yukl, *Leadership in Organizations* (6th ed.) (Upper Saddle River, NJ: Pearson/Prentice Hall, 2006).

3. W. Ury, *Getting Past No: Negotiating Your Way from Confrontation to Cooperation* (Rev ed.) (New York: Bantam Books, 1993).

Chapter 10 It Is Not Always About You

1. P. M. Senge and others, *Presence* (1 Currency ed.) (New York: Currency Doubleday, 2005).

Chapter 11 The Big Picture Does Not Exist until You Help Them See It

1. T. J. Erickson and others, *Gen Y in the Workforce*. (Boston: Harvard Business School Publication Corp, 2009).
2. P. M. Senge, *The Fifth Discipline Fieldbook: Strategies and Tools for Building a Learning Organization*. (New York: Currency, Doubleday, 1994).

Chapter 12 Ambiguity Is Their Kryptonite

1. P. M. Senge, *The Fifth Discipline Fieldbook: Strategies and Tools for Building a Learning Organization*. (New York: Currency, Doubleday, 1994).

Chapter 13 They Want to Know "What" before "Why"

1. Higher Education Research Institute, 2005. *The American Freshman* (Los Angeles: UCLA).
2. *Best places to launch a career: 7. teach for America—BusinessWeek*. Retrieved 10/31/2009, from http://images.businessweek.com/ss/09/09/0903_places_to_launch_a_career/8.htm.
3. Google web site, (2009). www.google.com/support/jobs/bin/static.py?page=benefits.htmlandbenefits=us#bbb.
4. G. Hamel, *The Future of Management* (Boston: Harvard Business School Press, 2007).
5. Towers Perrin Global Workforce Study, (2007).
6. B. L. Kaye and S. Jordan-Evans, *Love 'Em or Lose 'Em* (3rd ed.) (San Francisco: Berrett-Koehler, 2005).

Chapter 14 Building a Millennial-Friendly Culture

1. C. Benko and A. C. Weisberg, *Mass Career Customization: Aligning the Workplace with Today's Nontraditional Workforce* (Boston: Harvard Business School Press, 2007).

INDEX

A

Abrasive orientation, 36, 108–111

Adapting (adaptability), 25, 26, 33–34, *See also* Cultivating competency; Flexing (Flexing competency); Incenting (Incenting competency)

Advancement, opportunities for, 45

Affirmation, 95

Age cohorts, 16–18

Ageism and age discrimination, 37–46
  recent interest in, 37–38
  and stereotype threat, 39
  survey on, 40–46

Age norms (age norm theory), 19–20

Aging, global, 7–8

Aikido, 102

All-stars, identifying your, 155–157

American Sociological Review, 17

Apathy, 142

Argyris, Chris, 54

Attending to authority bias, 135

Attention, getting, 82, 83

Austrian, Sonia, 18

Authority, 5, 9, 27, 110–111, 156

Autonomous orientation:
  and bias of experience, 51–53
  as Millennial intrinsic value, 50–51

Autonomy (Autonomous orientation), 35, 50, 51, 57

B

Baby Boomers, 5–6, 8, 15, 16, 18–20, 31, 83, 95, 96, 109, 145

Befriending employees, 88–89

Belonging needs, 144, 145

Benko, Cathleen, 159

Bias, suspension of, 25, 33–34, 52, 158–159

Bollas, Christopher, 16

Boredom:
  anticipating, 75, 78
  with job description, 137

Brainstorming, 72

Broadening (Broadening competency), 36, 91, 120
  and consequential thinking model, 124–125
  and learning from success/ failure, 122–123
  practicing, 123–124

INDEX